Poison Heart

Poison Heart

Surviving
THE RAMONES

by

Dee Dee Ramone

with

Veronica Kofman

FIRE FLY

First published in 1997 by Firefly Publishing,

Firefly is an imprint of SAF Publishing Ltd.
in association with Helter Skelter Publishing Ltd.

SAF Publishing Ltd.
12 Conway Gardens,
Wembley,
Middx.
HA9 8TR
England.

The right of Dee Dee Ramone (Douglas Colvin) to be identified as the author of this work has been asserted by him in accordance with the Copyright, Design and Patents Act, 1988.

A CIP catalogue record for this book is available from the British Library.

ISBN 0 946719 19 5

Front cover photograph: Godlis

Printed in England by Redwood Books, Trowbridge, Wiltshire.

Contents

Our Thanks

Dee Dee Ramone thanks: The Ramones, Ira Herzog, Michael & Sally at Herzog & Strauss, Seymour Strauss, Veronica Kofman, Daniel Rey, Larry Schatz, Ed Steinberg, Seymour Stein, Harold Holloway, Dr Finkel, Dr Hanch, Stanley Bart, Western Union, and everybody who has stood by me in my life.

Veronica Kofman thanks: The Ramones, Dee Dee Ramone, Joey Ramone, William Norman Stone and everyone who helped.

Introduction

I am watching snow fall on New York City. I have just left Dee Dee and his new wife Barbara to enjoy the rest of Thanksgiving Day together.

There is happiness at the end of this story—a kind of peace and contentment. A new chapter has opened in a turbulent life. Dee Dee says that a Ramones story cannot have a happy ending. He may be right about that, but what you are about to read is not simply a Ramones story. It's about a life—the life of a man who was also happened to be a member of a world-famous rock band.

Dee Dee Ramone and I met again by chance in the summer of this year, on a flight to Los Angeles. I had not seen him for two years. We were both going to the Ramones' last-ever show. On the journey I read the first three chapters of this book, and I was hooked. It took Dee Dee five years to write his story. Every word was handwritten.

This is a disarmingly honest book about survival in a world that's full of false glamour, bitter betrayals and downward spirals. The other side of fame and fortune, from which very few emerge unscathed. Some don't survive at all. This seems an appropriate day to give thanks for those who did make it, and for their friendship and love. So good luck, Dee Dee, and

I know you won't mind me giving thanks also to your brothers-in-arms, The Ramones, for the happiness that you and they have brought into so many lives.

Veronica Kofman,
Thanksgiving Day
November 28th, 1996

On 2nd Avenue, New York City, 1976. *(Roberta Bayley)*

Chasing The Dragonfly

If there is a logic to this life, then I'd like to know what it is. I'm at the Chelsea Hotel in New York City again. I've taken a lot of drugs in this hotel. Now I'm going to get off drugs in this hotel. Strange, isn't it?

It's two weeks before my birthday. I am two weeks into withdrawal from methadone, which is the most addictive drug there is. This is going to be the hardest test for me, I can tell. It's going to be quite an experience. All the demons from my past are tormenting me.

They say that the Chelsea Hotel is haunted. I agree. A dragon fly is flying around in my room right now. A "she" dragon. Like Connie, one of my demons from a long time ago.

She flew into my room here seventeen years ago, didn't bother to knock; she just burst through the door yelling curses at me. Connie was very, very drunk. Eventually she passed out and slept it off; but before she did, she completely destroyed the place. She broke a champagne bottle on the radiator and tried to kill me with it—slashing at my neck with the sharp glass edges. Finally she exhausted herself and threw the broken bottle through the window, smashing it in the process. That was how Connie said good night: "Fuck you. It's over. Go to sleep." So I hit the sack.

In the morning we acted like everything was normal. We would get ourselves together the best we could, then go downstairs to the street and hail a cab to the Lower East Side, get out and go cop some dope from someone. This was 1974 or 1975. Connie was a go-go dancer. I was struggling in the Ramones. We were both dope addicts.

It's the beginning of the 90's now and I am fed up with it all. I am going to fight back. I give the dragon fly a look that could kill, but she shrugs it off. She's in a frenzy now, flying at me from behind, then changing direction and flying straight at me. Trying to sucker me to look into the light. Fuck that. That ain't gonna happen.

I am going to send every shitty memory I have of this hotel straight back to hell. I start a fire on the rug and come at her from behind. I set light to her head with another match, then watch her burn. Then I feel normal again. So I start to relax and stare at an unplugged fan, trying to will it to spin. Don't fuck with me. If you're experienced, I think you'll understand.

Deutschland Deutschland Über Alles

What I understand now is that I wasted a lot of effort worrying about nothing. Probably because I felt like nothing. My parents were horrible. Their lives were complete chaos and it felt like they blamed it all on me.

My mother was a drunken nut job, prone to emotional outbursts, where she would go spinning around the apartment beating her fists in the air, or falling down and hammering the floor with them so as to let everyone know that she was tough and not to fuck with her. She called herself Tony, which is about as silly as me calling myself Dee Dee, when you think about it.

Besides having a mom who was a lot like Connie, my girlfriend when The Ramones started in the early 70s, I had a weak, selfish drunk for a father, who was somehow like Connie too and somehow like the person I became. My mother met my father after World War II in Berlin, where he was stationed with the US army. They fell in love and got married. My father was thirty eight years old and my mother was then just sweet seventeen. By the time I was born, my father had become a Master Seargeant, and every two years or so the family had to move from one shit German town to another.

I have seen pictures of my parents' wedding in Berlin, and they were a very nice-looking couple. My mother was very beautiful, I'll give her that, and my father was a handsome man. Both of them had those frozen, faraway, vacant stares, though. I guess living through the Second World War had fucked them up in the head. Mom had experienced the bomb raids that left Berlin a demolished shell. Dad had fought in the Battle of the Bulge and later Hamburger Hill in Korea.

My mother was born on a Sunday in 1931 in Berlin, in a hospital built by Frederick the Great. She seems to have had a very restrictive life, even though Berlin was a big city with plenty of violent crime. She was two years old when Hitler came into power in 1933. Those were terrible times. The communists and the Nazis were killing each other and beating each other up in the streets.

At school, it wasn't easy for her. Every day my mother and her classmates had to pay allegiance to the flag. Hold their arms up in the Nazi salute and sing "Deutschland Deutschland Über Alles" and "Die Faderland". "Deutschland Deutschland Über Alles" means "Germany, Germany over everything" and is rumored to have been written by Horst Wessel, a Berlin pimp, who later became a Nazi.

By 1936, the Olympics were staged in Berlin and the city was so clean it looked like the streets had been gone over with a toothbrush. By the time the Second World War started my mother was eight years old, and along with it came ration cards and block wardens. The Jewish people were forced to wear a yellow star on their clothes. Then came the Krystallnacht, the night all the Jews were attacked in their homes and in the streets. My mother remembers the screaming. She was a little girl, and not against anyone. She was scared.

Then came three years of bomb attacks. Everybody aged fourteen to eighty four was ordered to defend Berlin. My mother was fourteen years old when the war ended. The city was full of dead bodies, everywhere. The river was full of dead bodies. My mother helped to bury them.

There was an indoor swimming pool on an army base in Berlin that I discovered when I was about fourteen.

"Mom, it's great" I told my mom about the pool. "Why don't you come swimming there with me and Beverly?", I pleaded.

"Oh no, Douglas, I couldn't."

"Why not, mom?" I asked.

"Because I remember that pool after the war. It was filled with the blood from the bodies of dead horses and dead people."

Some of my earliest memories date back to the time when I was six years old and living in Munich, Germany, on another army base. I remember a lot of wild drunken fights between my parents. Once, late at night, I was woken up by noises coming from the living room. I got up out of bed to see what was going on, and peered down the hall to check out the situation.

My parents were causing all the commotion. My dad was sitting on top of my mother, smacking her around. They were both yelling and woke the whole building up. In the morning, everyone acted like everything was normal. It was weird to me, though. I couldn't really understand why my mom would be throwing all of our dishes out of our fourth floor window. Or the times when I had to hold up mom's head in the hope that dad would pull over so she could throw up on the side of the road and not on me. My parents seemed so miserable that secretly I was hoping that dad would just run our little German car right off the road, and kill our whole family.

Mom introduced me to rock'n'roll, though. She was a troublemaker— but she dressed cool and had a Bill Haley and the Comets EP, and that "I'm going to Kansas City" record. This was the late fifties—you couldn't ignore the teenagers in pegged black chinos and greasy hairdos, boppin' around the Munich American High School, which was right near the building where I lived.

I tried to go to school, but I failed the first grade, so I was too embarrassed to go back, except at lunchtime, when no one would see me. I would hide in the bushes and spy on the teenagers hanging out with their transistor radios. This is how I could hear the music. I fell in love with rock'n'roll. It was exciting to me and seemed defiant. I liked everything that seemed edgy. Like going to see the movie "The Mummy" with my mother, or going to see "The Ten Commandments" on my own. The film was six hours long, so they had this weird intermission where they opened up the Exit doors so that everyone could go outside and smoke a cigarette or whatever. The contrast between the dark, safe, fantasy world in the movie theater and walking out into the blazing sunshine, where everybody could see each other, struck me as edgy. I worried about having my ticket stub to get back into the theater. "The Mummy" was crazier and sicker, but it was weird to see a complex film like "The Ten Commandments" on my own.

I remember thinking how thrilling it was when the cops brought Little Jimmy Preger, the local hood, into our building where we lived. He had passed out and they brought him upstairs on a stretcher. Jimmy had a "fuck you all for what you put me through" James-Dean-type-look on his face. He didn't care any more. He was sixteen and doomed—and he knew it. I was seven years old, and my prospects seemed pretty bleak as well.

My parents continued to drink and drink. They'd rant and rave until they passed out, which really embarrassed me. There was never any peace and quiet. Even at five in the morning, they would be having it out. Once I wandered into the living room in my pyjamas to see what was going on. I was in a daze, mom was going crazy again and I could see dad holding her down and yelling "Call Miss Preger". Miss Preger was Jimmy's mom and lived in our building. My mom was yelling for me to call the police. Finally, someone else did and the cops came and arrested my mother. She locked me in the basement before they took her away.

My parents had some wild parties. One night, some of their friends jumped off the balcony for a goof. I don't know what happened to them after that. Dad couldn't be bothered to explain it to me. He was too busy getting drunk all over again. My mom too. She drank highballs containing Four Roses bourbon, Coke and round ice cubes. They're pretty good, and make you feel like you're glowing.

It had gotten to the point where I had to avoid my father. It became too scary to come home. I spent most of my time wandering around the army base by myself. I had to live in a total fantasy world. The real world was too fucked up for me.

For a while in the early 60's, my family and I moved back to the States and lived in Atlanta, Georgia. My father got stationed there, so we moved into a little apartment near the army base. My mother named it "Bugs Lane". They don't have that many bugs in Germany, but it seemed our whole new apartment was infested with them.

There was an active social life for the families of the soldiers on the Atlanta base, so we would go there to hang out a lot and that was fun. The soldiers and their wives were young, mostly in their teens and early twenties, and rock'n'roll was blaring from the PX snack bar. This was where you could buy rock'n'roll records and transistor radios, Aqua Velvet aftershave and Gold Cup socks.

You could hear rock'n'roll at the swimming pool too. It seemed to go along with the sun, the comic books, and the potato chips. On the weekends, they had dances that had the top Twist bands. Mom, my sister Beverly and I would always be there. Once, outside a fairground in a suburb in Atlanta, my father and I were walking past a trailer that had a stage built next to it. A tent was pitched out back behind the trailer, and there were girls in bikinis, dancing to a live rhythm and blues band. It was pretty sexy. You could go in the tent and watch the girls strip, but my dad and I just kept walking. I was glad to keep moving, my father would only have caused an embarrassing scene.

Soon, my father was stationed back in Germany, when I was eleven or twelve. Pirmasens was a very violent, anything-goes kind of place. Everybody who lived there worked in one of the factories and a big cloud that smelled like a sewer hung over the place. If you lived there, you were sort of embarrassed to say so, because it was so rough. The population of Pirmasens was a mixture of wild American soldiers and their bored dependants, plus a lot of angry Germans. Germans and Americans don't get along too well.

I didn't have many friends. I never have. Around my building, the kids would sit on the swings and spit at each other. If anyone brought marbles or toy soldiers to the playground, the other kids would surely lift them. We were mean and hateful and all had the same problems—fathers who drank themselves to death and beat up moms, and both parents taking it out on us. You tried to make the best of it. Being miserable seemed normal. There didn't seem to be any other way.

It was in Pirmasens that I had my first encounter with violence. It happened between me and this other kid called Krudd. Like me, Krudd had a German mother, and his father was stationed at the army base. He was a mess sergeant and spent most of his time planning meals for the troops—his free time he spent over at the enlisted men's club drinking and playing the slot machines. Krudd's mother, on the other hand, was a real German "hausfrau" type. She resembled what the Germans refer to as a "putzfrau", which is a dirty, toothless hag that mops the stairways and is in one of those better-watch-your-step moods all the time. It's no wonder to me why Krudd was creepy. He could only be that way, especially since he was growing up in Pirmasens—he was guaranteed to be a loser.

Krudd was also on the minus zero status socially at school. He was not popular. He was also smelly and overweight. He was just a creep, and treated accordingly by the other schoolkids. So Krudd and I had something in common. Neither of us were popular. Both of us were losers.

But Krudd had one thing going for him. He owned a Framus Tobacco Sunburst folk guitar, that somehow became very rock'n'roll when he picked it up in his beefy mugs. It was all about the mystery of owning a guitar. No one knew how to play guitars too well to rock'n'roll music then, so I gladly put up with watching Krudd show me a few things on the guitar. He showed me "The House of the Rising Sun" in open tuning, which I tried to practice. But soon the guitar novelty thing wore off—I have a short attention span. It was my fault and I could sense Krudd becoming increasingly agitated with me. Then at school one day, just before class started, I was roughhousing around with him, and out of nowhere, he hit me in the face with his fist, and it knocked me flat on my ass. I thought the fight was over, the teacher was getting real angry and wanted everyone to sit down so he could start our lessons. However, according to the local code, I had to meet Krudd later for a re-match after school.

I had stuck my neck unwillingly in the noose, and now I had to go to my own funeral. I felt sick, but there was nothing I could do. After school, I entered into the center of a ring of jeering, unsympathetic spectators. I knew then that I wasn't a fighter, but I had to do this. All my theatricality and fantasizing wouldn't help me out of this one. It was obvious that Krudd was going to beat the shit out of me. He was meaner and bigger than me, and also he had already sort of beat me up an hour before. I couldn't let that happen again, and since he was too tough an enemy for me to take apart with kicks and punches, I did what I had to do.

I pulled a blade on him. It was a pearl-handled switchblade with a razor sharp four-inch blade. Weapons like knuckle-dusters and switchblades could be bought over the counter in Germany and everybody carried something. It was all part of it. This made Krudd back off in order to think about things more carefully. In a goofy sort of way, I was then able to take control of the situation. I bluffed my way out of it with a few thrusts and parries to the air, and by putting on that mean evil face that I know how to do. It was serious too—no one but my parents had ever hit me before. I was afraid of Krudd, so it was a good thing that he backed off. Needless to say, I lost his friendship too, but what did I care?

Also, Pirmasens gave me my first introduction to morphine. One day I found a whole bunch of these morphine tubes hidden in a garbage dump behind a garage. Some poor young GI must have been planning to use them, no doubt having become familiar with Skagg back home in the States. It was around this time that Elvis Presley was stationed in Germany and it is rumored that he first started taking drugs in order to stay up during guard duty on those long, cold winter nights. The morphine came in khaki-colored toothpaste tubes with a big needle screwed on to the end. You jammed the needle into your thigh and squeezed the dope into the flesh. I was unfamiliar with drugs then—it looked too sick to do that to myself at that point in my life. At first they might seem like a drag, because they came with such a big needle, but a dope fiend would ignore that as a temporary inconvenience and do them anyway. The needles looked dangerous and threatening, but I took them over to the playground to show them off to a gang of the other kids. Nowadays, if you could get your hands on stuff like that, you would instantly be a very popular person with freaks lining up outside your door, but it was unheard of back then.

Morphine is a heroin high in its more ancient form. A ticket to cloud nine where the kick is at its lushest. To get pharmaceutical ampulet styrets or phials of it is rare. Once, as I left the playground, I saw one of these styrets laying in the sand by the swings, so I brought a few of them home to show my dad. I was hoping it would make him proud of me for turning them in. When I got upstairs, he was there. He was acting like a caged animal and pacing back and forth in the small apartment. He seemed like he had a lot on his mind and was trying to hold back a lot of tension, but I took the risk and disturbed him.

"What are these, dad?" I asked.

"Gimme those."

He smirked and snatched them out of my hands.

"Where did you get this stuff?" he asked me.

"Oh, I don't know".

"Well, get out of here!" he told me.

So I left. He was really angry. Dad really hated drugs.

Somehow, even at the age of 12, I knew I was a loser. I couldn't see a future for myself. I thought the only thing I could hope to do was join the army. But, I didn't even make it for a week in the Boy Scouts. I was too afraid to ask my father any questions on anything, let alone ask him for permission to go on a camp-out.

Then I heard The Beatles for the first time. I got my first transistor radio, a Beatle haircut and a Beatle suit. It seems pretty crazy now, but this was 1963 and The Beatles were a big thing. I identified with these new rock'n'roll songs that were played on Radio Luxembourg, the pirate station that broadcast from the English Channel. They had Hubbly Bubbly commercials and played the Searchers, the Beatles and the Dave Clark Five.

My sister Beverly and I also went to see movies like *Blue Hawaii* with Elvis Presley and *The Parent Trap* with Hayley Mills. When the Beatles' film *A Hard Day's Night* came out, all the kids in the theater fell in love. You could feel it. We all came out of there glowing.

Once, around this time, I was taking out the garbage and found a box of old "Playboy" magazines in the trash bin behind where I lived. I took them upstairs and looked them over. There was an article about a wrestler called Gorgeous George which caught my attention. He seemed to be a bit of a maniac. Somehow, my reaction to that article inspired the name Dee Dee to me. He didn't seem like anybody else. I liked that. Before the Beatles got real famous they had called themselves the Silver Beatles instead of just the Beatles. I guess everyone wanted to sound glamorous. It was in style then, and John Lennon called himself Johnny Silver. George was George Perkins and Paul was Paul Ramone. I thought it was pretty outrageous to change your name to a made-up one, but I liked the idea. I was lost in another fantasy, and changed from Douglas Colvin to Dee Dee Ramone.

Rebels were a lot cooler to me than squares. My parents seemed like a continual drag. I could never forgive them for what was going on at home. I don't know, maybe mom or dad would have been happier if I'd beat up my sister Beverly all day and night, and started the morning with beer for breakfast, but by then I didn't care. I had my own scene.

I was hoping it would get better when we all moved back to my mother's home town of Berlin, but it didn't. So what? By now it didn't really matter to me. I had rock'n'roll and it gave me a sense of my own identity. I tried not to go home as much as I could and I spent my days shoplifting with my friend Robert at the big department store, Ka De We, near Wittenberg Platz. We also tried to rip off the antique shops around Nolendorff Platz for war relics to sell to American GI's.

Robert and I spent hours in old bombed-out buildings and vacant shell-scarred lots, searching for more war relics to sell to antique shops. Our favorite hunting ground was Potzdammer Platz, where the big Banhoff had once been, and where Hitler's bunker had been too. Once, I found a Nazi helmet that someone had soldered a handle onto. Probably so that they could use it to cook potatoes in after the war was over.

They put up the Wall when we had previously lived in Berlin. Before the Wall had been erected I can remember Beverly, my mom and I taking the S Bahn into East Berlin to visit my grandparents. In those days, instead of a refrigerator, they had a closet called a "kool schrank". Somehow, the milk in Germany didn't seem to go rotten like the milk in America. Their apartment was heated by a coal fire and my mother's stepfather had a little coal yard which was watched over by a German shepherd named Greif. In the day time, Greif slept under the kitchen table but you couldn't pet him because he would bite.

Later on it was forbidden for Americans to take the S Bahn. Robert and I used to ride the E Bahn under East Berlin, and when the subway train was in an East German station, it wouldn't stop; it would just race by and Robert and I would have our noses pressed against the window to make faces at the Vo Po's, who stood guard with Russian tommy-guns, like they did at Checkpoint Charlie.

Later on, when we moved to the American sector of Berlin, near Argentinisha Alle, I would walk Kessie, the family dachshund, in the mornings and pause for a minute to wave at the tanks clanking down Argentinisha Alle to the Grune A Wald. Then, at four o'clock the tanks would clank back up to the Argentinisha Alle to the motor pool. All the kids in the neighborhood would cheer them, and then it was time to go home for dinner.

No one was ever home at my house. Mom was normally with Beverly at the ballet school where my sister was taking dancing lessons. Dad was nowhere to be seen. So I was there, alone with Kessie. I would listen to the rock'n'roll on the Armed Forces radio shows, stuff like "Dang Me" by Roger Miller. Or I would go to the PX snack bar, where I could get a cheeseburger and a chocolate milk shake. I would also sit up in my room alone and read "16" and "Hit Parade" magazines about groups like the Monkees, Paul Revere and The Raiders, and also Dino Dessi and Billy. I would also try to play my Italian electric guitar which I had bought at the Music Haus Am Zoo near Ausburger Platz. I went there every day and stood outside and looked at the guitars in the window. The one I liked most was a green Sunburst Echo, with three white pick-ups and a tremolo arm.

The bands in Berlin played the Liverpool Hoop and the Berlin American High School. They would set up their Selmer PA columns and their Vox amplifiers and run through the hits of the day, like "Working in A Coal Mine", "The Midnight Hour", and "Gloria" by the Shadows of the Night. These bands were amazing. The best were the Hound Dogs, the Restless Sect and especially the Boots.

By then I'd begun to take dope. There were lots of dealers around the Braunhoff Am Zoo area. They would fill the hypodermic needles from big plastic bottles of liquid morphine. The German dope was strange, but it was fun. It felt like you were getting an electric shock when you shot it up. Then you went completely numb. I would have done it more often than I did, maybe three times a month, but I was too afraid of my father. Later, when I moved to New York, I got more serious about drugs.

Clothes were also high on my must-have list. Levi's jackets were in suede, yellow or cranberry. Hush Puppies came in pale green or baby blue corduroy. You picked up ideas of what to wear from many of the bands that played in Berlin around that time. I thought the Rolling Stones were the most edgy dressers. It was a great time for music and I saw the Troggs, the Kinks, the Small Faces, the Hollies, the Beach Boys, the Rolling Stones, The Who and the Walker Brothers.

Then one day I woke up and Berlin was plastered with pictures of Jimi Hendrix. He had an afro, was biting his teeth together, and playing the fuck out of a Fender Stratocaster that he was shaking behind his head. He was playing his first concert in Berlin. My mother, my sister and I left for

New York a few days later, so I had to miss his show. My father had gotten out of control once too often and we had to run for our lives.

The Summer Of Hate

A couple of weeks after leaving Berlin I was living in Forest Hills, Queens, New York. It was a good idea to get out of Berlin when we did. Having left my father, I thought things would get better, but they just got stranger. Somehow, I just couldn't relate to my new neighborhood. At least in Berlin you didn't have to be on alert all the time.

Forest Hills is one of those neighborhoods which is a subway ride to and from Manhattan—it's about twenty minutes on the F train and G local to 8th Street and Sixth Avenue. It is a nicely groomed neighborhood with lots of Coupes de Ville and Lincolns parked on the street. All the buildings are the same red brick color and chewing gum colored sidewalks snake through the area. There are little fringes of grass hugging the buildings where dogs go to the bathroom. In the mornings, the janitors would burn the trash in incinerators and a thick gray smoke would pour out of the chimneys. I loved it in the morning. As soon as I would hit the sidewalk, I would kind of catch myself and then peer through the morning confusion, on alert.

Kessie, our dog, whom we had brought with us from Berlin, would scamper out of the lobby, down the stairs to the street, her nails clicking behind her. I would stand lookout for her. Then, Kessie would change from the ready to the action position, squirt the sidewalk and bolt back into the building, while I was watching out for the police. They were so fussy. If you were caught letting your dog run off the leash, you could get a summons. The cops would ride around on motor scooters in the morning looking for trouble—blue knights in plastic armor. They were forever giving out parking tickets and looking out for kids who didn't go to school.

I started taking the subway to the Village in Manhattan. The first time I took it to the city, I got off at Roosevelt Avenue and had to ask someone on the platform next to me—"How do you get to Greenwich Village?" I felt so foolish, but I was headed in the right direction. It was easy. I just had to step into the F train.

It was a cool time in New York. I had read about the scene in the Village in "Hit Parade" magazine, so I kind of knew where to go. I went to check out the Night Owl, but it wasn't a rock club any more—they just sold day-glo posters. So, I went over to the Café Wha which was completely splashed in day-glo paint. There you could see live bands like the Raves, Cherry People and Kangro.

Although drugs were becoming a big influence on youth culture, they were still sort of a mystery. The message in the Village was "Turn on, tune in, and drop out", but at first I didn't know where to get any drugs. The Café Wha was where Jimi Hendrix had pioneered psychedelic music, but the atmosphere in there was so soothing that, when a good band was on, I felt completely like I didn't need anything else.

A month after we moved to New York, I took my first tab of acid. I met my new friend Egg on Queens Boulevard, and we each took a Blue Flat. Our other friends asked us if we had done it before, and we said "Yeah, sure". It was a beautiful trip and when I came home the next morning, even my mother seemed to be in a good mood, but she struck first.

"Douglas, you seem to be in a good mood. Why are you so cheerful this morning. What's up with you?"

"Oh, I don't know, mom" I said. Then I blurted out, "Oh, I just took some LSD last night with my friend Egg, and I am still tripping. I feel wonderful. Even the cereal looks beautiful. I wonder what's in those corn-flakes?"

"Well" she said, "let's listen to the new Jimi Hendrix album, Doug. It's called "Are You Experienced?" So I finished my breakfast and rolled a joint. I didn't bother to get any sleep. I had to be at Daitch Shopwell, the supermarket on 108th Street where I had just got a job, in a couple of hours, so I just sat there in a daze until my mom left for work. All I could think of was getting some dope from my friends at work to calm me down from the acid.

LSD was fun. I did it hundreds of times, but it really wasn't my thing. It was heroin that would get me through the day. Early on I could sense the big problem with narcotics was that they tended to lead to crime. If you use heroin, you catch a habit and end up a slave to the drug. Sooner or later you start to lead a double life and lie for drugs and dollars until you eventually become consumed by the whole experience and take on a new identity as a criminal misfit. Once heroin gets its claws into you, you'll end up doing anything, illegal or otherwise, to get a fix.

I have such a weak, criminal mentality, that my new criminal identity consisted mainly of making associates with the local hoods in the area, like my friend Jeff, who was already doing armed robberies and breaking and entering with this other guy Ricky and his friends. Jeff was a big kid for his age, and strong. I never saw him rob anyone but he used to come to the supermarket and show us the money he'd stolen. Then he would put some steaks under his jacket and just walk out. You couldn't argue with him, but he was a nice guy. Later on, he found Jesus while on acid.

After this, Jeff decided he didn't want to do any more robberies, and es-pecially not with Ricky's gang of friends. But, Ricky said that Jeff was too involved and it was too much of a risk to let him out of it. So, what they did was walk Jeff over the bridge into Flushing Meadows Park and killed him. They assaulted him, stabbing him over and over again, but somehow he refused to die. Finally, everyone left, Jeff was lying on the grass, bleed-ing to death, and that was it. I guess dying alone was the only peace he'd ever get. It didn't seem like he deserved to die like that.

Forest Hills was a pretty open-minded neighborhood, but heroin was more of a city thing, so I would cop it in Manhattan in the fleabag areas, and sometimes at the fountain in Central Park. I would buy a half load from my dealer in the park every day for twenty four dollars. This is when the dope in America was coming into the US from France. It came in glassine envelopes and was cut with quinine. I always felt like that's when we were getting the real stuff. After that, the heroin was never the same. It was strong and made you scratch yourself and nod out. A half load of dope was fifteen two-dollar bags. If I sold them, three were mine, but if I wanted to, I could get three dollars a bag for them in Queens, so I always sold some to my friends. When I went back to Forest Hills, I was making out pretty good.

I could already see America changing and I had only been there a few months. There was a lot of funky stuff going on. It was getting looser. In Central Park they started getting guys there on the weekend pushing supermarket carts around, stacked with beer cans on ice. You could get beer. Cold beer. Right in the park. Cop it like dope. In the liquor stores you could start buying wine that tasted like pop, so that kids could drink it.

Things were getting more outlaw. You could see street gangs like The Savage Nomads starting up in the suburbs, where they had not been seen before. Now they were coming on strong. One day the Nomads came into the park to fight another gang from the South Bronx. These guys were violent. They were saying one thing to everybody—Fuck You. Another time, I saw some of them hassle a dope dealer sitting by the band shell fountain. They whacked him with pool cues pretty bad. If that wasn't bad enough they also started whacking his Doberman.

I saw a tattoo of Jesus on a guy's shoulder during that summer. I was about sixteen or seventeen years old and didn't have any tattoos yet. In 1969 a tattoo like that was really weird. It was as outlaw as you could get. The ultimate way of saying "don't fuck with me." Later, I got that same tattoo as my own little way of saying I was sick of having to conform to everything, just because the Ramones had a look. When I went for therapy, it was something which I almost came to blows about with my psychiatrist, Doctor Jagger. I had to convince him to get it. What a laugh! I was a full-grown adult, and yet I was struggling to get his permission over something so stupid. I still think that's crazy.

1969 was the year of the summer of hate. For me, it wasn't about going to see Jefferson Airplane at the Central Park band shell and taking LSD. It was about sitting on a park bench drinking wine and snorting deuce bags of heroin.

I wonder if there wasn't some systematic plan from somewhere to fuck up people in America. Letting dope into the country on purpose to fuck up fools like me, who they saw as the burdens of society. It was well known that the CIA was on the side of the opium warlords, so they wouldn't sell out to the Chinese Communists and go red. And also because it's so profitable—drugs are money. And where did those orange tang methadone biscuits come from? Was it just part of the deal? It's a big letdown to be sixteen years old and already know that nothing's going to change.

I thought America was the land of equal opportunity, but I didn't have the ones that the other kids in Forest Hills had. We were all fucked up, but my situation was even worse. I was already a High School dropout, which was kind of lower class for Forest Hills. The key to survival seemed to be a college education, but I had already graduated to my role in life—that of social deviant. There wasn't much I could do about it. I am ok with it now, but back then I wanted to climb up the ladder to success. At least a little bit. I didn't feel that the supermarket was worthy of my talents any more. Also I couldn't live on thirty five dollars a week, so, after scanning the "New York Times" for a few weeks, I finally accepted a job in an insurance company, Employers Insurance of Warsaw, or something horrible like that. I liked working there, delivering the mail in the office every day.

Forbidden Fruit

By the early seventies, I wasn't bothering with Forest Hills that much any more, or my old haunts like the Café Wha or the Fillmore East. The scene had moved to midtown Manhattan and the Upper West Side. Disco music was was all the rage, and with it came the glitter clothes. The big thing then was the "Super Nature" thing, like Shaft and Superfly. The cool clubs were the Sanctuary, Tamerlane and Superstar. These were Harvey Wall-banger and Quaalude clubs—places to hang out until the small hours.

I was going out at night and going to the mailroom during the day time. I would go to work with coffee and a buttered roll from Chock Full o' Nuts, a copy of the "Post" and a bunch of loose joints to sell to the other guys in the mailroom. Sometimes I would skinpop milky-white heroin to cope with the pressure. Then I started mainlining it. The track marks sort of tattoo you, no matter if you've planned it or not. To get the money for my little dope habit, I would sometimes empty the change box in the soda machine at work and keep the cash. Or I'd take the subway instead of a cab when doing a delivery for my job. I was also selling dope to my friends. I could feel myself transcending into a sort of negative Jesus. Nobody wanted to see me around in Forest Hills any more. That was OK. They would all pester me for dope sooner or later.

Instead of hanging out in the parks around Queens at night, I was becoming a night owl around New York. Places around 48th and Lexington or around Central Park West like the Forbidden Fruit, a late-night juice bar for young deviants—somewhere hip where you wouldn't expect it. Girls that went there usually worked at massage parlors and took care of businessmen during their lunch hours or when they got out of work at 5. These girls would go to the Fruit to celebrate with their pimps. The club would be filled with Spanish and Italian kids doing the Hustle and the Bump. All the boys that went there tried to look cool and were always looking for trouble.

There were two big street fights outside the club during the few short months it existed. As the club was closing, people would start to mingle outside, hanging out on the sidewalk. The guys would break off car antennas and whip out 007 knives—always a favorite knife in New York. Everyone was all dressed up in platform shoes and glitter-disco outfits, making it even more theatrical. The action was so fast that it was quite breathtaking. One gang would run down the street attacking the guys on the other side. Then that side would retaliate scattering their opponents. It would happen in the street, between the parked cars, not on the sidewalk, and everyone would stuff themselves into this small space. You couldn't tell what was going to happen, because it was so fast and it was so crowded. When it cleared, there was always someone left lying on the pavement.

Another time outside the Fruit, I saw this big, loud-mouthed creep get stabbed. This guy didn't make any motions to fight or anything like that. He just stabbed the creep and ran. The creep just lay there moaning—"He stabbed me as I was getting out of there!"

It would have been nice if you could have walked out of the Fruit at closing time, straight past all the other creeps and into a waiting hearse. Then you could lay down in a coffin, close the lid, and be driven off somewhere. Better than trying to leg it to the 59th Street Bridge to catch the bus to Rego Park with some girl from Flushing that's just taken her shoes off and thrown them away. She's real out of it on Quaaludes, and can't walk very well. She's too much of a burden for me. It's just too messy and I am not in the best of shape myself. So, as the crowd from the Fruit fades, so do I. As I am walking away, I turn around to see what she is doing, and she flashes me the finger and a "Fuck you, Jack!" frown. She's not going anywhere—I think to myself that it's better if I leave her to her own devices. I am going back to Queens and that's not easy after a Friday night at the Fruit.

Thank God it's Saturday, I think to myself again. As I walk past Jumping Jack Flash, I give it the finger. It pisses me off because it's the store where I bought my cool white platform shoes with stacked heels, but they're killing me. I want to go home.

The bus lets me off on Queens Boulevard, near Rego Park, which is a bitch. I don't even want to think about the walk back to my mother's apartment from the bus stop. She lives on 66th Road, near the Hermits House. It's a long walk and I am dressed up in the shoes, satin pants and glitter top. My feet are sore and I am tired. Just another creep in the smoggy city, trying not to acknowledge the new day. The sun doesn't feel warm. It's not innocent like the sun in upstate New York, in the country, on a Saturday morning.

Instead, this sun comes up opaque, trying not to be seen. It's more comfortable in the dark, lurking near subways and below the buildings that tower above Manhattan. It gives me that unfocussed feeling like how I feel about modern technology. I have the long walk to nowhere to look forward to. It's ok. It doesn't phase me. People like myself aren't supposed to be going anywhere. If there's a bit of paranoia in the air, then that's fine. How else could it be? I didn't exactly want to go home. Not when I was caught short with no dope, no money, and going into withdrawal.

Then my mother yelling at me as soon as I walk into the apartment, and there's me, shaking with cold even though it's summer, sick because I need some heroin, and in no mood for any bullshit from anyone, least of all from her.

Mom doesn't seem to be aware that this might become a bad scene. She's so used to these types of dramas that she reacts to it in the typical way she's always seen it done. She picks up a pot of old spaghetti off the stove and flings it at my head, splattering the wall with rotten meat sauce.

"Cut it out, you creep!" I shouted at her. "That could have been my brain splattered on the wall instead of spaghetti."

That was all the excuse she needed to completely freak.

"You bastard! Coming home on dope! I'm going to kill you!"

She picked up my treasured Echo guitar and held it over her head in the battle axe position, and then got right down to serious business, chopping up the furniture, everything, the lamps, the records, the record-player.

The whole time she's doing this demolition job on the apartment, she's yelling at me "I hate you! I hate you! I'm going to kill you!" Then she started shouting "You're just like your father!" That really pissed me off.

But I wasn't afraid of her any more, especially since my father was still in Berlin. So I decided to go at her like dad would, and for the first time I yelled and cursed her back.

"You old German hag! Get the fuck out of here, you whore cunt!"

I thought she was going to shit herself. She looked really frightened and left. She ran right out the door. I had never seen her make a decision so quickly before. Never. Even though it was her apartment, for once I think she did the right thing. I wasn't going to take her abuse and yelling any more, so I gave her a taste of her own medicine. I wasn't an innocent, defenseless child any more, so she was really risking it. I never asked her for anything, she was too crazy. By then I was a vicious creep with a lot of hate in me. I guess my mother realised that, so she ran for her life. I wish I'd punched her in the face. I picked up the Echo and trashed the rest of her apartment instead. Then I threw the broken guitar through the living room window, slammed the door off the hinges and left. What else could I do? Walk her over the bridge to Flushing Meadow Park? Still, if I got angry with someone, I would go for the throat. I thought that was normal.

Why do you think I ended up in the Ramones, who were described as a barrage of white hate?

The Boy Met Johnny

People who join a band like the Ramones don't come from stable back-grounds, because it's not that civilised an art form. Punk rock comes from angry kids who feel like being creative. I guess that's why members of the Ramones were known to throw TV sets from the roofs of apartment build-ings at people below on the street. We had a special hatred for old ladies pushing their carts full of groceries home from the supermarket. In Forest Hills, you would find used TV sets on the sidewalk every day, when the janitors in the area put the trash out on the street to get picked up in the morning. It was great. When they hit the street, the tubes exploded on the concrete and they scared the shit out of people. It was something to do.

When you're sixteen years old, angry and bored, you have to be very creative to stir up some excitement. Like those dried up old Christmas trees the janitors would put in the basements after the holidays were over. The kids in my neighborhood would sneak down there and set them on fire. Then they would run back out to the street and stand there and laugh.

By then I had become a manic depressive. I was hopeless. I could only laugh at someone else's expense and I thrived on negativity. I can see now how it was only natural that I would gravitate towards Tommy, Joey and

Johnny Ramone. They were the obvious creeps of the neighborhood. All their friends had to be creeps. No one would have ever pegged any of us as candidates for any kind of success in life. But that's how it goes.

The Ramones were the elite of the rebel class in Queens during the late sixties and early seventies. Definitely not High School student, college material types. Instead of school and homework, we were into goofing off and fantasy-making. All of us were a bunch of ill-mannered low-lives. We thought cripples were funny because you could goof off on them—like it was lucky to rub a midget's head, especially if the midget was bald. I was off-the-wall enough to see some kind of logic in those kinds of superstitions.

If I had to run with anyone in Forest Hills, then it had to be with an off-the-wall type or worse. When I first met Johnny Ramone, it was at the top of the hill on 66th Road, near the Hermits House. John was delivering dry cleaning from the cleaners where he worked. That was his full-time gig. Later he worked as a construction worker at 1633 Broadway, in the same building where I worked as a mail clerk. John's hair was real long then. Down to his waist, like Mark Farner from Grand Funk Railroad. He had on tie-dyed jeans and a tie-dyed headband and those same cheap Keds that he still wore even when our band got famous and we had money.

John was always very friendly to me and eventually we started talking about guitars and amplifiers and stuff like that. I started telling him a fantastic story about the equipment that I owned, probably like the one Bill Wyman must have told Mick Jagger and Keith Richards to get into the Rolling Stones. I said I had a twin Sound City stack and a plush amp with a two eighteens cab. Actually I played my Hoffner Beatle bass through a friend of mine's amp. It was a real old ampeg, with one eighteen inch speaker. It's hard to describe that amp. It was sort of embarrassing. No one knew how good they sounded then, because they looked so weird. I blew up my Vox Pacefinder or Escort or whatever they were called, a 10 watt amp with an eight inch speaker. I kept the Vox at my mom's apartment, but it was ruined from using it with a boss tone to dirty up the sound.

The Who had just played Central Park and John and I liked them then. Pete Townshend had smashed up all these Sound City amps. Later, Townshend got those cool Sunn amps like the Stooges used.

John is a very strong-willed person. He was one of the first friends I made when I moved to America and our friendship was based on music. When I first told John that The Stooges were my favourite group, he said he liked them also. I couldn't believe it. Someone else in Forest Hills liked the Stooges besides me. It was like a miracle. To me, the Stooges were the most real rock'n'roll band around. They were the best. The original Stooges, with Iggy, Ron and Scott Asheton and Dave Alexander. They were very, very creepy. Creepy is the best description for them. They were the kings of the creeps.

John was always way ahead of his time. He wasn't biased about music, he'd give anything a chance. But he had his tastes. He liked outrageous, loud, raunchy rock music. He was older than us and seemed to know a lot of other things too. He would tell us sick stories, trying to hip us up and we wouldn't have a clue. He would tell us stuff like how he'd been to see the Yardbirds at the Anderson Theater and the first Rolling Stones concert at the Academy of Music. He'd thrown rocks at the Beatles when they played Shea Stadium. John also liked Ted Nugent, the MC5 and Black Sabbath. He had seen Black Sabbath's first show in New York at Steve Paul Scene.

We both loved Jimi Hendrix. John saw him play at the Café Wha back in 1966 or 1967. He said it was quite an experience. Jimi had apparently played a guitar that was completely broken off at one end of it—it didn't phase him one bit. When he broke a string, he didn't stop playing. A Stratocaster is hard to re-string anyway, but Hendrix could put a new string on his guitar while still playing. Finally, he threw the Strat over his head into the Fender twin, and it snapped in two. Then he cooed into the mike that everyone should go over to Central Park tomorrow to see him play. He was opening up for the Young Rascals, and he told everybody he was doing the gig to get a new guitar.

Johnny Ramone never broke a guitar. He couldn't be bothered. He found one he liked and always played the same one. A Mosrite like the Stooges used. Except for the strobe tuners, Johnny Ramone never spoiled himself. He made the most with what he had. That's what I liked about him then. Still, it's sort of strange to play sick music on a Mosrite which is really supposed to be a surf guitar. Somehow they're alright to use with fuzz tones and stuff. They also go very well with bowl haircuts.

John was always doing things his own way. He had a big guitar amp speaker, and a tiny Sony tape recorder, and somehow that was his stereo. Richie Stern and him had a lot of tapes—they would sneak cassette players into concerts and make tapes of bands. They'd bootleg things for us, like if the MC5 were playing, or the Stooges.

Richie lived in Lefrak City. He was a very special person, a big Stooges fan—a very crazy supermarket clerk dope-fiend type. He would play Stooges tapes for us and do Iggy impersonations by the light of the glowing TV set. Then he would sing things back to the tape. I'd sit there on the floor and watch him with amazement. Richie was a weirdo and originally we wanted to have him play bass in the Ramones. We had one rehearsal with him, but he refused to join because by then he had started working at OTB. He had put thirty five hundred dollars in the bank in seven months. Not bad for an eighteen year old creep from Lefrak City.

Home Is Where Hell Is

Seeing Joey Ramone in Forest Hills then was a weird sight. Joey was very tall, and had a red afro hairstyle, modeled after Jimi Hendrix's. It was called the Explosion and was the sort of haircut you could get at Paul McGregors' in the East Village. Joey looked like a druggy. He could usually be seen wearing a yellow suede fringed jacket from Paul Sargent's, cranberry corduroy trousers from The Naked Grape, moccasins instead of sneakers, and those freaky round tinted glasses that he still wears today.

Joey was my drinking partner. We would buy a bottle of wine, put it in a paper bag, and sit on a stoop drinking it. My mother really liked him, which is strange. She would get so excited if he ever came over to see if I was home. She would always say to me, "Oh, Joey came by", but she wouldn't tell me if anybody else came by. And she would always be asking me questions about him. I told her I didn't know myself. Later I was surprised when he moved by Union Turnpike and had his own apartment. I don't know how he did it.

Then there was Ira Negel, one of our friends who lived in Forest Hills. Ira was a bass player and the owner of a brown "perfecto" motorcycle jacket. He was a big guy, kind of a goon-with-a-big-heart type. He had a puffy face and was a big complainer. In the end he couldn't join the band—his mother wouldn't let him. But Ira's mother was actually cool, so it was OK. She didn't mind if all the kids hung out at her apartment, smoking pot instead of going to school.

Then, there was the mysterious Tommy Ramone. He called himself Scotty then. Scotty was a made-up name like Dee Dee. Tommy was quite a fantasy maker. Maybe coming to the US from Hungary made him appreciate the simple things—he certainly had more gratitude than most people. I was more self-destructive. I couldn't see the sense in trying to make anything work if I could break it. For a while I used to live with Tommy in Debbie Harry's apartment. I had to admire how Tommy would place importance on the need for decent, human, rational survival, unlike anyone else in our group of friends. Tommy would go to the store and buy himself some hamburger meat and potatoes and cook them, trying to make himself a meal, and I would be laying on a mattress with half a pint of blackberry brandy, watching him cook. I just couldn't relate to that at all—forget it. But it's a good quality for a roommate to be like that, rather than to be like I was.

By the time Tommy was seventeen, he had been through one series of bad luck after another. The story goes that a gang of kids in Forest Hills put Tommy (Scotty) through some sort of humiliating experience and he became very nervous after that. Once he insisted that we get up and leave a House of Pancakes on Long Island without finishing our meal. No one knew why.

He had a girlfriend called Claudia and they were both heavy smokers. Nobody wanted them smoking in the van. Later, Tommy couldn't stand it in the van for 10 hours, not having a cigarette, and everybody giving him an attitude about it. One day he just said, "Forget this guys, goodbye. I'll go smoke where I wanna smoke."

Forest Hills was starting to make me nervous as well. It got so that I had to take a couple of reds and drink a pint of Gallo wine before I took the walk down 108th Street to Richie's parents' apartment in Lefrak City. I was completely happy when I sniffed a tube of glue or a bottle of Carbona—it took you out as far as you could go. When I was high I would call special phone numbers to listen to the beep beep beep. Things would go buzz buzz buzz buzz. Sometimes, someone would come back from the supermarket with stolen cans of whipped cream. We used to huff the gas from the whipped cream cans to heighten the effect of the Carbona and the glue.

Finally the Stooges came to New York. There was an ad in "The Village Voice" that they were coming. They had a gig at the Electric Circus, which is where they have the Narcotics Anonymous meetings on St Mark's Place nowadays. I went to that Stooges show with my girlfriend Linda and my friend Egg and his girlfriend Bennie.

Iggy didn't seem to like New York. He told everybody off. He had come on real late because he was shooting up heroin backstage and couldn't find a vein to get a hit. Iggy was famous for his dog collar, silver elbow-length gloves and red underpants, but when he finally came out on stage he was only wearing his underpants. He threw a can of silver paint over himself and then rolled around in a bunch of glitter. Then he threw up on the floor and lay there in the vomit, rubbing it on himself.

Scott Asheton, the Stooges' drummer, had a big Nazi sign painted on the back of his motorcycle jacket. They were loud and angry. It was a great idea. They played the same song for twenty minutes that night. Once in a while they would stop. Then Iggy would shout "Take it!" and they'd do it again. It had only two chords in it and the only words to the song were "I want your name, I want your number." Then someone shouted "It's the ghost of Mick Jagger!" Iggy seemed upset by that remark and he walked off. The Stooges didn't come back to New York for a long time.

My first car was a Volkswagen bug. I was still living in Forest Hills and saved up the money for it by working in the mail room. Richie Stern, Johnny Ramone and I all had jobs. We were trying hard to save money. That was our little revenge on society.

When my mother found out I wanted a car she was happy. She thought I would drive her to Rockaway Beach in the summer or something, so she suggested that I write my father a letter and ask him for the money. I did, and he wrote me back a "fuck you" letter. That was the end between him and me. He was a useless bastard and I hated him, but I don't know where I was coming from asking him to buy me a car. Christ, that was stupid. My mother was stupid to suggest it.

As usual, I was on my own, so I went to the newsstand on 66th Road by the Trylon Movie Theater and bought a copy of the "Buy Lines". I thumbed through the foreign cars of the Automotive Section. Egg had warned me to get a Dodge Dart or Chevy Nova, but I wasn't listening. I was going to do it my way, but I didn't know anything about cars. I had a license, but I didn't know how to drive yet. I didn't know how to fill a car up with gas, change a flat tire or open up the trunk or hood. Nothing.

The female police officer on my driving test felt so sorry for me that she didn't even make me take the test. She passed me and sent me on my way with a "Have a nice day, kid!" I ran into her again years later. We were both pretty tipsy. We were in a bar. We got to talking and she confessed that she only passed me because she was hoping that I would get killed in a car accident and get to end my miserable life a little bit sooner.

"Boy, it's too bad you're still around!", she added.

"I know, life has been tough on us both", I replied, stumbling out of McCann's Bar & Grill to the Lexington Avenue F Train that goes back to Queens. It would have been nice to take a taxi instead of the subway once in a while, let alone own a car. What a grim existence.

I know now that I should have listened to my friend Egg and bought a Chevy Nova or Dodge Dart, but I bought a Volkswagen. It was already fucked up when I bought it from a guy in Elmhurst. When I got it back to Forest Hills I knew that it was a lemon when the bastard thing wouldn't start up again. I got right on the phone and called up Tommy, because he was an expert on everything. A little while later, Tommy pulled up in front of my Volkswagen in his Dodge Dart. Then he ended up re-charging my battery. After he left, I drove over to the carwash on Woodhaven Boulevard. I pulled up to the entrance and gave the dude there the money.

I didn't know what to do; the attendant couldn't speak English, so he couldn't tell me. So I drove the car right into the tunnel. It was completely dark in there, so I whacked right into the spinning brushes, which knocked the car off the track and broke the windshield. All the soap suds spilled into my car. It was pretty extreme. I had just smoked some Mowwie Wowwie marijuana and I was buzzed. The Volkswagen was rolling down the tunnel, spinning off the tracks, and I ended up being knocked unconscious. I don't know how, but somehow I had got them to replace the smashed windscreen with an old Volkswagen front window, and vacuum out the soapsuds. It was still slouchy in there, but they also re-charged the battery so that I was able to put-put the Bug home to Forest Hills, where I parked it in front of the Hermits House.

Tommy, John and I would go sometimes with Tommy's friend Jeff Salem to clubs on Long Island and to a bar called Nobodies in the West Village on Bleecker Street. Sometimes we would go in Tommy's Chevy Nova, but since I had a car, everybody wanted to go out in my car, so one Friday night everybody met me in front of the Hermits House. I didn't know it, but Tommy was tripping. After driving a few blocks, everybody made me pull over. They had a quick conference. Tommy got out of the Volkswagen, circled around the car and got behind the wheel. It was a roller coaster ride down Queens Boulevard. Everybody was stoned and yelling. Johnny Ramone had the Stooges' "Live at the Electric Circus" on full blast on the tape deck. Finally we were getting on the 59th Street Bridge and Tommy was getting red in the face. He was exasperated.

"Hey, guys, can you lower the music?" Tommy said. "I am tripping on LSD. Those Stooges songs are freaking me out. You don't want to run me off the road."

That was like the signal for things to get worse.

"What's the matter, Tommy? You don't like the Stooges?"

Ho, ho, ho. I lit up a joint of Chiba Chiba Colombian Gold. I was having a good time until I noticed a burning rubber smell. It was the car, not the marijuana. The car was on fire. The electric system had gone, and smoke was pouring out of the engine, which, in a Volkswagen, is in the back. Everybody started shouting with glee. In two more minutes, the car stopped running completely. Since the rest of the 59th Street Bridge is on a downward angle, we were able to coast into Manhattan anyway. We left the car on the sidewalk, where it had smashed into one of the Bloomingdales windows on 59th and Third, crushing the dummies in the store window to death. We continued our journey when we caught the F train at 53rd and Lexington to 8th Street and Sixth Avenue.

Eventually I moved to Manhattan because it's such a hassle to go back and forth from Queens to the city. I got a small walk-up apartment on 85th Street and Second Avenue, and I got a new pet dachshund that I named Glenda.

When I started taking drugs, my manic nervous energy turned from nervous twitches, tapping on tables with pencils and making coo coo bird noises, into inspirations for songs. I was prepared to take LSD, speed and grass if necessary. My mind was like a time bomb anyway. Ready to explode, with demons lurking about the edges of it to protect me from reality. I was composing all through my pre-teen and early teen years in this way. I had the heavy wah wah, screeching feedbacks, vocal melodies and all the drum parts to hundreds of songs written out in my mind. It was all mental. I filed them all away in my head, locking the parts together to form the first songs I ever came up with. These were power rock songs. My musical abilities were too limited at the time for me to compose any other way. It was all in my imagination.

None of these songs will ever be documented, but it was a good way for me to dream myself out of the daily grind. One of the songs I wrote at this time, maybe my first, was called "I Can't Do It":

I can't do it
I can't do it
I can't do it

I can't change tomorrow
At the stairs to hell
I can't change tomorrow

I can't do it
I can't do it
I can't do it

I can't hold on to my hand.

Another song went like this:

Home is where hell is
Home is where hell is
Home is where hell is

And now I am home
I am with my friends
Having a good time
Have a tube of glue
Take a tab of sunshine

Home is where hell is
Home is where hell is
Everything's so bright
Everything's this way
Everything's this way
It's going to be alright
It's going to be alright
Tonight
Tonight
Tonight!

A bad breakdown inspired me to write "Questioningly" which I composed on a folk guitar, and then insisted on playing it for my mother after I had it worked out.

"Mom, mom" I shouted into the living room from the hallway of her apartment in Forest Hills. "Can I play something for you?"

She listened to me play it as we sat in front of the TV set. I could tell that she was very surprised that I could write a song.

"How did you do that?", she asked me.

"I don't know", I said.

Then I wrote my first punk rock song on my solid body electric guitar. It was an old K solid body guitar which I bought at one of those pawn shops on 8th or 9th Avenue. I took that guitar with me wherever I went—from Brooklyn to uptown Manhattan, from Forest Hills to Queens. The song was called "I Don't Wanna Get Involved With You". In the next year or so I experimented with a few different musical projects and I also started writing more songs. I soon came up with "53rd & 3rd", "Loud-mouth", "I Don't Wanna Go Down to the Basement", "Now I Wanna Sniff Some Glue" and "I Don't Wanna Walk Around With You." They just kept coming out.

Sometimes I would go back to Forest Hills to see Johnny Ramone and Joey. I tried to start my own band in the city, but that didn't work, so then I answered an ad in Andy Warhol's "Interview" magazine for a guitar player for the Neon Boys, a band featuring Tom Verlaine and Richard Hell, but it wasn't what I wanted. Later, when Richard Lloyd joined them in Television, they were really good.

When the New York Dolls were playing in Manhattan, it was Beatle-mania all over again. Every creep in town started a rock'n'roll band. I was really happy seeing the New York Dolls playing. They inspired some kind of rock'n'roll feeling in me. We thought Johnny Ramone was a good guitar player. No one else did at that time. Tommy was very particular about that kind of stuff and had a real dislike for Johnny Thunders because of his guitar playing. But I liked Johnny Thunders for his guitar playing and his songwriting. But the thing that impressed me most was his harmonies. Like on "Chatterbox", that Minnie Mouse harmony thing, I always liked that. But I don't think I really realised how great he was until the Heartbreakers started. I think because his image was so great in the Dolls, that I forgot about how good he was.

Before the New York Dolls broke up in 1973 or 1974, Malcolm McLaren had come over to New York to try to rescue them. He put them in red patent leather and booked them at the Hippodrome, a club in midtown Manhattan. In some ways it was their most professional gig, but it didn't get them anywhere—booze, broads and bad luck had already killed them off.

After the Dolls split up, the little rock'n'roll scene in Manhattan died out a bit and it was hard to find anywhere to play. Lenny Kaye, Buzzy Linehart and Patti Smith played Max's Kansas City, but that was about it. Then Television started up and it paved the way for the Ramones and Blondie.

The Ramones, CBGB's, 1977. *(Godlis)*

Take it!

Johnny Ramone and I really had no intention of ever playing in groups again. We both had bitter experiences of other groups we had been in before the Ramones started. We were happy just taking the subway to work every day, going to Chock Full o' Nuts and to the Metropole for lunch to watch the go-go dancers and drink a beer.

Joey had a band called Sniper. He was trying to break into the New York "glam" circuit that was happening around then—groups like The Harlots of 42nd Street, The Fast, Teenage Lust and Kiss. Tommy (Scotty), Jeff Salem and Monte Melnick also had a group called Butch with the drummer from Dorian Zero.

The glitter look took a lot of upkeep and the gear was expensive. We would get custom-made snakeskin boots sent from England via Granny Takes a Trip in New York. Johnny Thunders and Tommy Ramone both went to London to get the right stuff to be the top flashmen about town. Johnny Ramone had an exact replica of the James Williamson outfit with the leopard collar that James wore in the Stooges' "Raw Power" stage. John also had silver lamé pants from Granny Takes a Trip that he wore for the first few Ramones gigs.

Joey and I would sometimes hang out in this unmentionable dive on Queens Boulevard called Gildeas. Every time we went there I would get very drunk. I don't know how Joey got me home. Home was crashing on the floor of his mother's art gallery on Queens Boulevard near the Trylon Movie Theater. Joey's band Sniper used to rehearse there in the basement of the store. Once Joey bought some fruit and vegetables at the grocery store and used them to do a painting. He churned them in a blender and painted with them—you could either look at the painting or eat it. He was quite the artistic type. He also liked to tape thunderstorms on a reel to reel tape recorder.

I went to see a Sniper concert once when they performed with Suicide somewhere in Manhattan. It was a weird night. They did a cover of the Rolling Stones' "Let's Spend the Night Together". Joey was called Jeff Starship then. Forgive me if I don't have it exactly right. Could it have been Jeffry Starman? Well, it was a long time ago. Anyway, he was wearing pink patent leather trousers, a silver lamé top, a pink feather boa, custom platform boots from Granny Takes a Trip, and he was singing into the mic like he had been doing it all his life. It was quite impressive.

When I first saw Alan Vega and Suicide, I pulled out my 007 knife and palmed it behind my wrist. To be frank, I was a little worried. If Iggy had created a Frankenstein, it was Alan Vega. When Alan jumped into the sparse audience, it was a bit too much for me. I didn't know what was going to happen. He's a very serious performer.

Later, Joey and I went to Max's Kansas City to check out Suicide one more time. No one was there that night but Joey, me, and a beautiful blonde in heavy S&M gear. About six or seven minutes into Suicide's set, she walked up to the right side of the stage next to some huge speakers and stood there frozen in space. The noise and the atmosphere were pretty tense. It was buzzing and flashing. Then the girl started smacking her head on the speaker cabinet, breaking the flesh. Blood was coming out of her head and she kept doing it, over and over, really hard. Eventually she stopped and just stood there with blood dripping down her face, listening to Suicide play.

Finally the Stooges came back to New York to play. They booked a show at Max's Kansas City, but had to cancel. Iggy had thrown himself down the stairs and cut himself pretty badly with a broken bottle, because he wasn't happy with how things were going.

Around this time we started to take our first baby steps as The Ramones. Like a lot of the New York groups, we took our inspiration from going to see the New York Dolls at the Oscar Wilde Room at the Mercer Arts Center and the Diplomat Hotel in Times Square. After the Dolls broke up, there were still a bunch of creeps who needed a scene.

I guess it's only natural that Joey, Johnny, Tommy and I would start a band. No one else was exactly welcoming us with open arms into the Forest Hills musical community. They said we couldn't play. Years later, Johnny Ramone and I would laugh about how someone like Doug Scott, a local guitar player in Queens, could play Led Zeppelin's "Dazed and Confused" at sixteen years old and still never amount to anything. I couldn't even play the Stooges' "No Fun" and I achieved fame and fortune in the music business.

By then, even Johnny Ramone was impressed that things were happening in New York. Then one day, instead of going for lunch at the Metropole, we went over to Manny's Guitar Store on 48th Street to look at guitars. When we were walking down the street, John and I ran into Mickey Zone from The Fast. We told him we were going to take the plunge.

We ended up with a Dan Electro bass for me and a baby blue Mosrite for John. John tricked them at Manny's like he did the waitresses at Chock Full o' Nuts. We took them back to Queens, Johnny with his Mosrite stuffed in a Granny Takes a Trip shopping bag, and they became the guitars we started the band with.

Tommy and Monte Melnick got a rehearsal for us at Performance Studios near Max's in Manhattan. We tried to figure out songs from other records, but no dice. I still don't know how we got it together. I had no idea how to tune or play a bass. Eventually Johnny would show me the bass parts to my own songs, because I had absolutely no idea how they went on the bass. All I knew was the E.

Initially the band was me on bass and vocals, John on guitar, and Joey played the drums. The first time we tried to play, we waited and waited for Joey to get ready. Finally we just started cranking it out. I was so drunk I fell over backwards and whacked my amp. It started fizzling and then stopped working. We did our first show with The Fast at Performance Studios. For the second show, no one came back.

Monte was fed up because we were so messy, but he let us come back once a week to rehearse. Eventually he became our sound man, and then tour manager—he didn't want to be called road manager. Our first manager, Danny Fields, gave Monte the job of tour manager after our first big out-of-town gig at the Tomorrow Theater in Youngstown, Ohio in June 1976. We first met Stiv Bators and the Dead Boys that night. It was a bad night—we had about 10 people there. Danny said if Monte got us the money—$750—he could be tour manager. We got paid.

Joey had written some songs, like "I Don't Care", "What's Your Game" and "Here Today, Gone Tomorrow". He ended up becoming the lead singer because he knew the words. We then asked Harry, the drummer from Dorian Zero, to join the band, but he wouldn't play with us. That was a rank on the Ramones, but we shrugged it off. Tommy started playing the drums because no one else would do it for us. It was a last-ditch attempt to salvage a so-far unsuccessful musical career. Tommy completed the original line-up. After one of our early rehearsals, Tommy and I went into the studio office and had a talk. "What do you think we should call the band?" he asked me. "Oh, how about The Ramones?" I replied. I wasn't that serious, but the name stuck. Then everyone in the group took Ramone as a surname and we became The Ramones.

The next gig was with Blondie, who were called Angel and the Snake then, and with the Savage Voodoo Nuns. It was first time we'd played at CBGBs and we weren't ready for it. Tommy had booked us there. It was a let-down. It didn't seem as glamorous as Max's or the Mercer Arts Center. When we loaded in for the soundcheck, we had to watch out for rat, mice and dog shit on the floor. It was the pits. Especially Hilly Kristal, a big fat guy, who ran the place and apparently never bathed. His wife, Karen Kristal, managed CBGB's and hated the Ramones more than she hated CBGB's. It was very aggravating and very unfriendly. As soon as you walked in off the street, the smell of fermenting beer was so powerful that it made you want to walk out backwards. They didn't have any toilets, so the audience just pissed where they stood.

The first show we did there was OK. The place was filled with drag queens who had spilled over into CBGB's from the Bowery Lane Theater. They were great to us and helped us through the show, sort of making believe for us, and it was very cabaret-like. The audience were making catcalls, wolf whistles, and clapping dramatically to each act. It must have been a lot of fun to have been there that night. The Ramones were a very theatrical group then—like a play set to loud, sick music. We had two Mike Matthews amps from Electro Harmonics set up on chairs. They had four tens in them and were very hot-roddish.

When we sauntered on stage, I plugged in my bass and took a look around through the grim stinky haze in CBGB's. There was an ugly full-length poster of Marlene Dietrich pasted on to one wall next to the stage. The audience looked like a bunch of glowing Jack o' Lanterns sitting on a graveyard fence on Halloween night. We played about fifteen minutes and were a success. We were trying to go from one song into another. After a mishap, someone would go "Take it!" and I'd count one, two, three, four, and we'd stumble into another number. At the end of the show, I threw my Dan Electro up into the air and let it bounce up and down a few times until it broke. I thought that was the ultimate glamor.

Connie

I got drunk after our gig at CBGB's and as I was leaving the club at four o'clock in the morning, I noticed this babe sitting by the Bowery on the hood of an old car, filing her nails. I liked her right away. She was wearing a black evening dress, spiked high heeled shoes and had a bottle of Blackberry Brandy in her purse. She looked like an ancient vampire countess. Her name was Connie and her mission was to capture my soul, which she did. I spent the next few years depending on her, while the Ramones were getting famous but not making any money. We were both a lot alike—totally nuts. She was just as crazy as I was. We got kicked out of everywhere we lived because of our violent arguments.

Connie had an apartment on the first floor of a brownstone building on 16th Street. She was a little older and wiser than I was, and tried to look after me, but I was difficult. You couldn't trust me and I had to be checked up on. It was must have been exhausting having me for a boyfriend. Connie put up with a lot from me, but she was also a well-known troublemaker. She was always starting fights.

Not long after I met Connie, she started up with one of my ex-girlfriends in CBGB's. Blondie had been playing, and it had been a fun night, but Connie had to ruin it. She and the other girl ended up ranking on each other and shouting terrible names at each other. I hate spectacles, so I made a quick exit out the back door, taking one of my other girlfriends, Elaine, with me. Elaine was used to battling with Connie. They had been doing it for years over Kane, the bass player for the New York Dolls before I'd met either of them. Once, the two of them squared off on 11th Street, when Connie caught me sneaking around with Elaine. They were both tough girls and this looked like it might become more than a verbal row.

Elaine and her mother lived in a beautiful block on 11th Street, near St Vincent's Hospital. Once in a while they let me crash there, but I was getting on their nerves already. I could tell. I drank too much beer and raided the liqor cabinet one too many times. Elaine's mom could only take so much and finally she had had enough of me. There was trouble in the air, so Elaine took me for a walk over to Smiler's, the deli on 13th Street, to get some Colt beer, which was the strongest beer you could get in the States.

Connie stepped out of nowhere as we were leaving the deli. She was swinging her handbag around her head like Bruce Lee and she had put a brick in it for effect. She wasn't kidding around. Connie and Elaine went right at it, started manoeuvring for the best position and were shouting at each other. This was at the end of the glitter period in New York. It was 6.30 in the morning and we were very dressed up. I had been at the Eighty Two Club in the East Village and had been getting into hassles all night. It was quite dramatic. Then suddenly, Connie and Elaine both turned on me, Elaine grabbing me by the collar, saying "Dee Dee, do you want me or Connie?" Then, without waiting for an answer, she punched me really hard right on the side of my head. It sent me down the sidewalk and I busted open my chin when I hit the kerb. Connie thought that this was very funny, so with her bloodlust satisfied, but still slightly annoyed, she took me back home.

It wasn't long before we were thrown out of our apartment on 16th Street and home was now in something called the Village Plaza. The walls in there were painted a creepy lime green like the paint jobs in mental institutions and police stations. It smelled like green roach spray and was much more horrible than the Chelsea Hotel. Even most of my low-life friends wouldn't stay there. They would stay at The Earl, where Connie and I had already worn out our welcome.

We were making our lives much worse than they had to be. Connie was dancing at the Metropole, the go-go place on 48th Street. My job was to get dope for us. We would spend one hundred dollars a day on dope if we could. I'd go cop around Rivington, Suffolk and Norfolk Streets—side streets around Houston in the East Village towards Delancy Street.

Sometimes Jerry Nolan, the former drummer for the New York Dolls and I would go cop together. Jerry sometimes got dope for this weirdo called Dorian Zero, who lived uptown near where I used to live, near Third Avenue in the Eighties. He also always had a steady supply of Dioxin, a speed that you could shoot up and get with a prescription from a doctor. You put Dioxin in a little glass bottle with water and closed the lid, then you would put that in boiling water for a minute and let it cook up. Then it was ready to shoot into your vein.

Dorian could hit his parents up for money, so sometimes we would hop into a cab with him up to 48th Street to a restaurant that his father owned. That was the start of the insanity. Then, with the meter still ticking, we would head deep into New Jersey to complete the whole picture. We would end up in front of Dorian's parents' house in Cherry Hill. His parents were wealthy and connected. Their home was expensive and had seven acres of manicured lawn around it. It didn't exactly have a welcome sign outside, though, and it made me nervous. The whole deal made me nervous. Dorian would leave us outside and then go into the house to argue with his mother. We could hear him shouting terrible things at her. It would remind me of fighting with my mother, except that I never got any money from her.

For a while dope was called Chinese Rock in New York. When you would walk around the Lower East Side, people would smirk at one another on the sidewalk and let you know with hand signals that they had the

Me, Tommy, John, and Joey at our usual hangout
Thornycroft, Queens, 1975. *(Bob Gruen)*

The photo for the first album cover came from this shoot taken in a playground near 1st
Avenue and 1st Street, 1976. *(Roberta Bayley)*

Chinese Rocks. "The Rock". It was supposed to be good luck if someone had rocks. I must have had a lot of luck.

Jerry Nolan and Johnny Thunders used to call me quite frequently. Jerry would come over to my place to pick me up and then we would go cop some dope. The Heartbreakers were just getting together with John, Jerry and Richard Hell. I guess those guys were all dope fiends then. It was not easy to cop dope. It was unreliable, it was annoying and there were rip-offs. People would buddy up and go cop. If you went and copped for someone, you were entitled to "tap" the bag. Richard Hell had mentioned to me that he was going to write a song better than Lou Reed's "Heroin", so I took his idea and wrote "Chinese Rocks" in Deborah Harry's appartment that night.

I wrote the song about Jerry calling me up to come over and go cop. The line "My girlfriend's crying in the shower stall" was about Connie, and the shower was at Arturo Vega's loft. The intro to the song was the same kind of stuff I had put in songs like "Commando" and the chorus of "53rd & 3rd". I wrote these songs before "Chinese Rocks" and The Ramones had already performed and recorded these tunes.

By the time I got the song finished I was living on 10th Street. Jerry Nolan would come over as usual. It was perfect because the dope spot had moved to 10th Street and Avenue D, so my new appartment became a meeting place because it was so close to the action.

When Jerry was over at my place one day, we did some dope and then I played him my song, and he took it with him to a Heartbreakers' rehearsal. When Leee Childers started managing them, and got them a record deal, "Chinese Rocks" was their first single off *LAMF*. Leee was originally a photographer who took all the pictures that were on the wall of Max's Kansas City. He also managed Wayne County. The song did well too, and helped start a career for The Heartbreakers. It was dedicated to the boys on Norfolk Street, I can understand that, but the credits are false. Johnny Thunders ranked on me for fourteen years, trying to make out like he wrote the song. What a low-life manoeuvre by those guys! By then, I was really too fucked up to care.

Being a dope addict was the worst. It was never any fun. It gives a person every reason to be miserable so you have every excuse to do it again. Connie was only adding to my misery and I was starting to be glad when she wasn't at home and was at work, dancing at the Metropole.

A friend of mine then was Black Randy, one of the most hated punks in California. Randy would fly back and forth between Los Angeles and New York, in a Brooks Brothers three-piece suit. He was robbing these people for dope money and doing very well at it. He was a freak, a dope fiend and a con man. The Wall Street image was a front. I would always get Randy some dope when he came by for a visit. Because he was overweight it was always hard for Randy to find a vein when he was shooting up, so it would be messy, and I would end up miserable every time he came by.

Once Randy came over to the Village Plaza with a big wad of cash. I went to Rivington Street on my bike to cop for him. All the Puerto Rican dealers were sitting on the stoop checking me out. I was a customer, so they left me alone. I felt alright around Rivington and Norfolk Streets, but it wasn't my neighborhood and I was risking it being there. But that's where the dope was.

These cop spots were store fronts that the dealers turned into social clubs. They were painted in blood red, day-glo orange and green colors. There were day-glo devil heads painted on the walls. They would glare at you from under the black lights. Somehow these places reminded me of the Café Wha. It made it weird to cop.

The dope was sort of going along with the decorations. It was cut with procaine. The word was that it was from Mexico. It was brown rocks. Chinese rock. But they were saying it was South American. Clever, but silly. It was just a delusion to make it easier to get the dope into America from Thailand or wherever. It wasn't as refined as the old dope. I wish whomever was manufacturing it would have kept the dope a little smoother. We had to take what they had, or be sick, so we took it. Shooting up the dope with procaine was like shooting up heroin while you were rushing on glue. I knew that's what I would be in for, but I copped two bundles anyway.

One for Randy and one for myself. Then I rode my bike back to the Village Plaza.

Soon Randy and I were really stoned. Then Randy seemed like he was overdosing. I was very fucked up, in a heroin and procaine daze. Randy could have died. I should have called the police, but instead I poured water over him, using the garbage can under the sink for a bucket. It worked, thank God, and soon he started coming to, but by then the whole room was flooded, which would be a dead giveaway to Connie. When Randy woke up, he was pretty confused. The first thing he said was "Dee Dee, got any dope?" That's how it was.

Later, when Connie came home from dancing at the Metropole on Broadway she was pissed off.

"Dee Dee, what were you doing in here? You don't even have to tell me, you motherfucking bastard. You've been doing dope without me! This whole room is flooded. What the hell happened here?"

She didn't wait for my answer. In a flurry, she picked up a wine bottle, broke it over the radiator, and slashed me with it. It was a deep wound. There was blood all over the place. I held a towel over the cut and somehow made it to St. Vincent's to get stitched up. I took the stitches out later by myself.

A couple of weeks later, I got a blade stuck in my chest. I was trying to get away from these two guys, but they pushed me into a hallway. I was walking away as fast as I could, being as cool about it as I could, but they overtook me. "Narcotics control!", they shouted in my face. That stunned me a little, but I reacted with caution and said to them, "Show me your badges".

"What are you, a wise guy?", one of them accused me. Then they shoved me into the hallway of a vacant building. Both of them had German cat knives. One of them said "Should I stick him?" The creep he was with said, "Yeah!" There was nothing I could really do about it. I was just glad they didn't kill me.

A friend of mine had a loft at 6 East 2nd Street, around the corner from CBGB's, so it was very convenient for the Ramones. Mostly for Joey and me. There were three lofts in the building and a factory on the first floor. A crazy painter named Jimmy lived on the top floor. Below that was a loft that six drag queens from San Francisco called "home". On the floor below that lived Arturo Vega. Arturo had had bricks thrown through his windows so many times because of bad dope deals and crazy love feuds that it's a wonder no one ever got conked in the head by one.

Behind the building was a graveyard that had been dug up by the city. Some of the corpses had been buried upright in the brick wall. Once I went down there to get a loose brick, and a dead person's hand fell out of the hole where the brick had been. The hand was all bone, but a gold and diamond ring was still stubbornly stuck on its finger. It was an old engagement ring that some sucker must have bought this broad. The diamond must have been at least two and a half carats and the money I got for it at the pawn shop kept me in dope and hostess cupcakes for months. A lot better than the nickel bag I got twenty years later for my wedding ring on 10th Street after I left The Ramones.

So, I wasn't doing so well when The Ramones started. We were playing CBGBs over and over to survive. We kept saying we wouldn't go back but we had to.

To keep my spending on dope down, I tried to keep on the Flower and Fifth methadone program, a twenty four day program in New York. All my creepy friends autographed the cork bulletin board for the staff. Eventually everybody was on that program. Johnny Thunders, Sid Vicious, Nancy Spungen, me... Most of these people are dead now. I don't want to start counting or thinking about that. I don't know how I am still alive after all the drugs I used. I am glad they had that program then. For whatever it was worth, it made my miserable life a little bit better being on it. But this kind of lifestyle sucks.

Nancy Spungen was a go-go dancer and a groupie for the Heartbreakers. Everybody slept with Nancy once, and then dumped her. Then no one wanted her around at all. She could really get to you. Once, Connie tried to set me up with Sable Star, Johnny Thunders' girlfriend, while she was in Boston go-go dancing. But I went off with some other go-go dancer that I met at a Neon Leon show at Max's. Sable wasn't that hot.

I don't remember how well I really knew Nancy. Everything happened so fast. Connie knew Nancy first, because Connie was an ex-Dolls groupie and had been around more than everyone else. Everyone had a mutual fondness for drugs, sin and violence. The sicker the better. Like one day we went to go cop some dope like we always did, but we got ripped off. We lost our dope and our money. We were all dressed up and made ourselves look too conspicuous. I was in full Bay City Rollers gear, and Connie was in hot pants, platform boots and a halter top. We almost started a riot on 10th Street. I was glad I had dumped my platforms a couple of months before in favor of Keds sneakers. The monster boots like Slade, the Dolls and the Wombles wore, were impossible to run in. Connie was such a pro that she had no problem with wearing platforms—which for her could also double as weapons.

We ended up by the Gem Spa on St Mark's Place, huffing and puffing, out of breath. As we were regaining our composure, Nancy Spungen walked up to Connie and me. She seemed very miserable and started trying to bullshit us and get our sympathy. What a laugh!

Everybody was screaming, and soon we started to walk towards Chelsea. Nancy had an apartment on 23rd and Ninth Avenue. It was on the first floor. It might have been borrowed from a trick, I don't know for sure. Soon we were all stoned. Then Nancy gave Connie money, and Connie hopped a cab to 1st Street and Avenue C. I stayed with Nancy to case her apartment or whatever, and to get a free lunch out of it. When Connie came back from copping, we all got stoned again, and then we ended up in bed and tried to do some bad things. I don't think it ended up too special, though—it's all a blur.

Connie also stole Nancy's silver dollar collection. Connie was a clever dope fiend, always scheming to make more on the sneak. Nancy was younger and just learning then. She had a big crush on Jerry Nolan, but Jerry totally ignored her. He let Nancy buy him a few bags of dope, but that's about it. She was too much of a hassle. Also you could get a bad reputation hanging out with Nancy. On the bathroom wall in CBGB's there was some bad shit written about her by the other girls, who all hated Nancy.

Sometime around then I escaped from Connie with a girl that lived in the loft above Arturo Vega's loft. We both wanted to get away from 2nd Street and found an apartment in the "Village Voice" rental ads. I picked it out. It was on 10th Street, right in the dope area. Even though we were going out together and living together, I still didn't know much about her. She started going to some "job" every day. It was strange, but fine with me. When she was at work, Jerry Nolan started to come over to do dope and then he started bringing Johnny Thunders over.

One day my girlfriend stayed home. No matter—she was a big Johnny Thunders fan and was thrilled when John and Jerry came over. Thing is, though, she od'd on us. We had to strip her and toss her in a bathtub filled with iced water. Soon, we sort of just forgot about her. Later, when she came to, I was the only one there.

"What happened?" she muttered in a daze.

"Oh, I threw you in the bathtub" I answered her back.

"You didn't do this in front of Johnny Thunders, did you?"

"Yes, I did!" I shouted.

Later we were in bed and she rolled over and tried to hug me. I automatically jumped right off the mattress and that did it. She went crazy and started yelling "Fuck you, Dee Dee! Fuck you! Fuck you, Dee Dee! You never let me kiss you! All you're interested in is dope!" She was right. We broke up soon after that and I went back to the loft on Second Street. Arturo took me in. I was really glad to be back at the loft. All the commotion on 10th Street was too much already.

Arturo Vega was like the Ramones' evil mom. A mean Latin queen that tried to pass himself off as French. Although he was really Johnny's friend, initially he let Joey and I crash in his loft and it was sort of like home for a while. Joey had a notebook where he would jot down all these ideas for songs like "Christmas In The Crypt". He also wrote "Succubus". At rehearsal me and John looked at each other with a "what kind of language is that?" look. I only found out twenty years later that it meant some kind of monster woman.

Anyway, I think Joey wrote like me. I don't think he knew anything really about guitar chords, or the verse, chorus and intro. Somehow he just banged out these songs on two strings of a Yamaha acoustic guitar and then Johnny Ramone would struggle his best to interpret it. Johnny would show me the bass parts to my own songs because I had no idea how they went on the bass. But it came out very strong when we all did it, so I guess we knew we all had shortcomings and that's why John and Tommy couldn't give me and Joey all the songwriting credit. But Tommy Ramone wrote "I Wanna Be Your Boyfriend" and we could have made a million dollars on it, because the Bay City Rollers wanted to do it. But that's another story. I remember with "Listen To My Heart", after I showed it to everybody and we agreed to do it, Tommy said, "Oh, it doesn't have a middle eight in it". So I just wrote the middle eight on the spot. Tommy couldn't believe I could do that.

Anyway, I would be at Arturo's loft if I was nowhere else. I knew Connie would go there to look for me with a peace offering of dope. I slept there on a mattress that Arturo put for me in a corner behind the Ramones banner which he had hung up to divide the loft and give himself some privacy from Connie, Joey and me. Arturo ended up with Joey and me twenty four hours a day. He put up with a lot of craziness but he was crazy too. Eventually I think he formed a permanent resentment towards me—which lasts to this day. We will never shake hands or be friends or anything. But back then he was trying to put up with it for the sake of art. Yes, art. He was some kind of a mad, but very talented, artist. And very cool too. He saw punk as some sort of a brand new canvas to splash paint on. He became the Ramones lighting director, t-shirt designer and graphic artist and toured with the band for a long time.

My friend Egg had been over when I was out, and was leaving New York to move to Cleveland. He had come over to say good-bye, but I wasn't there, so he left a candle that he had made himself by the bed. What a treat, I thought, when I saw it. Egg left me a present. Wow! I was in such a good mood. I also remembered that I had a very, very powerful thorazine pill that my counselor at the Flower and Fifth methadone program had given me for an extra special treat. Connie had warned me not to take it, and was watching me, so I had hidden it until she went away. I am set tonight, I thought. I have my candle and my pill. This is great. I lit the candle and took the pill and polished it off with a modest pint of Gallo port.

I felt happier than I had been in some time, but my happiness didn't last. I don't know what was up with that candle, kind of like putting a hat on the bed. I don't know, a curse, a mojo, whatever. But it was negative, not cool, and it sucked. I realized my other girlfriend, Elaine, was in there with me. I was too weirded out to be romantic or kiss and was just quite content to lay there in a daze. Shortly, though, Elaine informed me that Connie had joined us. She was in there as well, and feeling lovable. I don't trust her, I thought. The thorazine had knocked me for a loop, and I was helpless. It was extreme and there was nothing I could do. It was like being in a straight jacket, so I just grinned that grin that I do when all is not well.

Soon it got worse. Elaine and Connie were pissed off at me and not paying attention to the candle which had melted and set light to the floor. Before we knew it, the fire started spreading throughout the loft. Connie was beside herself with glee and jumped up and started throwing cans of paint around to fuel the flames. She threw a can of paint at me, then splashed one of Arturo's paintings.

"Everyone gets a paint job!" she was shouting. "We're all gonna die!" She was thrilled. Then I thought I saw Elaine sneaking up behind Connie and trying to push her into the corner of the loft that was really ablaze and where the floor was caving in. But Connie was too quick for her. It was horrible. "Why me?", I was thinking to myself. That creep, Egg, who had given me the candle, had moved to Cleveland.

Sometimes it seemed never ending and I was stuck there to deal with one problem after the next. Like Jimmy, the demented drag queen downstairs. What a bastard. It's a wonder the building didn't burn down a million times because of the low-lives he was bringing up to his loft on the top floor. Bricks would sometimes sail through his window too, like the ones through Arturo's. It was weird, but it was bold, exciting, great.

Besides being a queen, Jimmy was also an artist. He was even crazier than Arturo Vega. He was a big boozer and a real sick guy or a girl—to him, it was the same. One day his wife came home and found him in drag. The bastard was lying on the couch dead drunk and stoned. He had a wedding dress on and eye make-up, blusher and red lipstick and a blonde beehive bouffant wig. He was quite nasty. The shouting started right away. You could hear it from Arturo's loft and from down on the street, where a crowd was gathering to listen.

"Queer motherfucker!"

"Fuck you, Mary!"

"You wish!"

"Get lost, sister"

Finally she left and we never saw her again. Everybody on the street let out a big cheer. Jimmy then came to the window and promised a big party for all to celebrate his good fortune.

After his wife left, Jimmy made good on his promise and threw a party like he said he would. He invited all the bums on the Bowery. It turned into a heavy drug and booze scene. Then he took some thorazine and completely lost his mind. He turned control of the household over to a brute called Margo, a very highly feared and tough drag queen who specialised in ripping off sailors on the Bowery and holding up drug addicts in the neighborhood. It all went downhill on 2nd Street from that time on. Having Margo for a neighbor was a curse. She was really horrible, so noisy and creepy that I started to feel like life wasn't worth living. The little building I called home was turning into the pits. I was getting paranoid. There goes my security, I thought. This can't last much longer. They're gonna come and throw us on the street any minute. Arturo was a wreck.

Connie said that if she had to fight Margo, it would be like a cat on a dog, whatever that meant. It was frightening and things in our building were definitely getting worse. There was a killing. A couple of them—stabbings. They were killing cats up there, I know that for sure, because they would throw their half-eaten carcasses out the window. It was disgusting.

Then Jimmy ran out of money. He got stuck up there with no more booze, no heat in the building because the city turned off the gas and electricity because he hadn't pay the bills. All his creepy friends started to get angry. Jimmy's guests were all real down and out alcoholics and perverts. No one gave a shit. They were all chopping up the furniture for firewood and building camp fires on the floor for heat and to cook rats they caught when no one had a cat. It was nuts.

Finally Jimmy convinced everybody that he had hidden a lot of cash behind one of the bricks in the wall. So everybody started aimlessly chopping holes in all the walls. Finally they stubbornly started searching in the basement for the money. After a while, Margo went down there to see what was going on. I didn't go down there to investigate what happened. All I know is that I never saw the rest of them again. I didn't ask Jimmy about it because he was too busy getting drunk and I didn't ask Margo because I always tried to avoid her even though she liked me. Leave well enough alone, I thought.

Finally Connie gave me the ultimatum. She had come at me with a butcher's knife the day before. Somehow I had reached out my arm automatically and grabbed a broom handle in my hand, and I managed to sweep the blade from Connie's left hand. I don't know how.

"Now listen here, sweetie, Connie. Please darling, please calm down. Please keep the knives in the kitchen. No more stunts today, ok? I am drained. I can't take any more. I am really tired."

Connie looked at me with glowing yellow hateful eyes. A look that could stop a cop.

"Dee Dee, you queer motherfucker", she shouted at me.

"Connie, what's up?" I shouted back at her.

"Well, Dee Dee, you stupid creep, what do you think? It's that fag Margo upstairs. I can't stand it. Fuck everything! I need some dope now to cope. I hate it! Do something, now!"

Above:
With Richard Hell at Max's
Kansas City,
New York. January 1976.
(Roberta Bayley)

Left:
A Ramones autograph
signing at Free Being
Records on 2nd Avenue
and St. Mark's Place in
February 1977
(Roberta Bayley)

I knew I had to face Connie or face Margo. What a choice. At times like this, I just lose all feelings in me. I marched out into the stairwell. I had on a heavy pair of jackboots and kicked a post from the railing to use as a club. Then I walked into Jimmy's loft—without knocking or anything —and sorted Margo and those freaks out. But that experience left me played out, and when Connie threw a beer bottle at Mark Mendosa, the Dictators' bass player, at CBGB's, the next day I went back to Queens to rest and hide out for a week.

Life started getting even more insane every day. It's a good thing for me that The Ramones started touring. We were doing shows in little towns in the American North East states most nights. That gave me a chance to avoid the East Village for a while. It got too hard for me to keep up a dope habit, so I switched to booze. Then all I had to deal with were my hangovers—instead of making it back and forth from Norfolk Street without getting stabbed, ripped off, or arrested. Basically, I was turning into a junkie. I think the Ramones really saved me, got me off the street.

Every musician I knew from that time said the same thing—"Oh, I was so happy when we started touring, I had somewhere to live, in the hotel every day". But then when it stopped, there was nowhere to go. Nothing to eat. The Ramones were like my family and my security. I could go and get a meal and a place to live and a place to play, and it was good.

Even early on, my relationship with the rest of them was always strained because I think they couldn't understand me. I probably threatened the security of the band because of my wandering traits. I wouldn't conform to anything. Everything immediately outlived its value to me. I don't know how it could have been any different. There was no one to show me any other way.

I never had a childhood. I couldn't have a band. I had to get somewhere to live. I was trying to set an unobtainable standard for myself and I think what set me apart from John, Joey and Tommy is that they seemed to have something I didn't. I don't know what their real family life situations were like, but I felt like an outsider, because at the end of the day, I really didn't have anywhere to go, and they did. Tommy wouldn't even let anybody in his apartment. He didn't want anybody in there. He would answer the door and peer at you from behind the door. You had to wait outside. John's parents were always really friendly to me. I really got along with them. His mother and father really liked me. But I always thought the other guys had a security that I didn't have. I had no place to go and grow up. I think that's why I had to have a secret life of my own.

I suppose I formed very bitter resentments towards the other guys. I felt like I shouldn't have been around them and they shouldn't have been around me, but we were stuck together. And the person who always made it worse was Johnny Ramone. But I know I caused a lot of trouble, a lot of grief. People caused me a lot of grief. It's nobody's fault. No bands get along.

A Trip To England

The Ramones had begun to make a name for themselves in New York City and were playing regularly at CBGBs, Max's Kansas City and other underground venues. Seymour Stein signed us to Sire records for the sum of $6,000. Seymour was a very smart man. He invented the theory behind selling alternative music and starting alternative labels in the US. He started by buying back publishing and putting out bands like Fleetwood Mac and the Climax Blues Band, and using the money from that to put into bands like The Ramones and Talking Heads, and later Soft Cell and Madonna.

The first album only took a couple of days to record in February 1976 at Plaza Sound in Radio City Music Hall. It was released in April.

The reviews were good, but sales of the first LP were not exactly spectacular, and because of our reputation, many promoters were still reluctant to book us. We made a far greater impact in England where the album quickly reached number one on the import chart, thanks to regular airplay on John Peel's evening show on Radio 1. One British critic even hailed us as the saviours of rock 'n' roll.

I guess the climate in the UK was much more inclined toward a band like the Ramones. The UK punk movement, centered around The Sex Pistols, was about to take off.

We flew to England in July of 1976, the weekend of the Bicentennial, to play two shows with the Flamin' Groovies. The first was at Dingwalls and then on Independence day, July 4th 1976, we played to 2,000 enthusiastic fans at London's Roundhouse, our largest audience so far. I remember it was a very hot summer in England that year.

Danny Fields, our first co-manager, showed us around town. Danny was a photographer and a member of the Warhol set, and he had also managed the Stooges and Jonathan Richman. He was friendly with Linda Stein, wife of Seymour Stein, owner of Sire Records, who also co-managed the band.

Our first look at London consisted of walking around Hyde Park at four in the morning. It was very low budget stuff. That's how Danny showed us around town.

Then we were on our own. I went off to Camden Market where I bought all the Doctor Feelgood and Eddie and the Hot Rods singles. I also bought "Keys to Your Heart" by the 101'ers. It was very exciting for me to buy these records. They were on weird labels that no one had heard of, and had cool picture sleeves. It was still so in touch with proper rock 'n' roll. The Rock On stall had a Teddy Boy feel to it. It was like being in a time warp seeing this fifties rock'n'roll scene and then to be opening up for the Flamin' Groovies, who dressed head to toe like the Beatles.

It was at the first show at Dingwalls, a small club in the middle of Camden market, that I got my first introduction to English punks. At the soundcheck I met Mick Jones and Paul Simenon from The Clash. Paul had paint flecks on his shoes. It was artistic, in a graffiti-style way. They all had short hair, but didn't seem mod. Johnny Rotten and Sid Vicious were also there that night. It wasn't my favorite show that we played in England or anything like that, but it was a great start.

The next night we played the Roundhouse with The Stranglers and the Flamin' Groovies. As we were driving up to the Roundhouse for our soundcheck, someone said "There's Sid Vicious!" Through the permanent drunken haze I was in I could see Sid standing by himself on the sidewalk, looking a bit off in space. It cheered me up to see him, somehow. He was a show all in himself, standing there outside the Roundhouse, wearing baggy red loon pants, a black fishnet top, eye make-up, black nail varnish and short blue-black hair that wasn't spiked up yet. I met him later on that night and we hit it off immediately. Sid liked the Ramones and started following me around. Later when he joined the Sex Pistols, he started wearing ripped jeans like Joey Ramone and a Ramones-style leather jacket.

The Ramones kept playing England so much around then that it's hard to keep it all straight. But I think the next time we were in England was in 1977. On a day off I can remember going to Brighton to see The Clash. It was one of the first times I had heard reggae music. I remember this strange sight of a thousand punks on the dancefloor, dancing between band sets to this reggae music blaring from the disco. I'd never seen anything like it before.

I was having a good time until I ran into Nancy Spungen on the balcony of the theater. She started shouting enthusiastically in my ear about Sid this and Sid that. She said that Sid was the star of the Pistols. That Sid was her new boyfriend. I couldn't hear The Clash at all because Nancy was shouting in my ear about Sid. It was too much. I became exhausted by all the commotion. I started entertaining the thought of pushing her off the balcony. Nancy ended up buying me off with a bottle of brandy.

The next night there was a party at the Country Cousin on the King's Road. The place was hot and there was no air-conditioning. No matter how much cheap warm wine and beer they dispensed to the party-goers it couldn't seem to quench their thirst. Everyone was drinking themselves silly. It was pretty decadent. I noticed Captain Sensible, the bass player from the Damned, as soon as I walked in. He was sitting at a fancy, expensive piano, and threatening to play it for us. He was dressed in a ballerina tutu and old Doc Marten's that someone had spray-painted white. Everyone was there, from Gaye Advert to Marc Bolan. I couldn't find any dope, though, until finally some German gentleman that I met at the party laid twenty grams of speed on me. I didn't know what to do with it at first. Then, with Sid trailing along behind me, we headed to the toilet to figure it out.

There was vomit everywhere. On the floor, in the sink, and overflowing from the toilet bowls. This is sick, I thought to myself. Sid and I both immediately threw up as well. I hadn't seen anything yet, though, not until Sid produced a horrible syringe with old blood caked around the needle. I gave Sid some of the speed and he tapped it into the syringe to load it up for a hit. Then he stuck the needle into the toilet and drew up water from the bowl into the hypo so he could coldshake the speed that was in the outfit. The water had vomit, piss and snot in it. Sid didn't seem to think that this was in any way out of the ordinary. His main concern seemed to be to shoot up and was prepared to put up with any amount of discomfort for the rush. Now I've seen it all, I thought.

While Sid was finishing his shot, John Cale walked into the bathroom. He was stinking drunk, but could tell right away what we were up to. He tried to be coy.

"Dee Dee, got anything?" he asked me in a friendly, nonchalant way.

"Oh, I don't know" I replied, lying through my teeth. "Ask Sid. Sid has some."

The next thing I knew, Sid was shaking on the floor having a fit. Green foam was coming out of his mouth. His eyes were popping out of his head. It was terrible, so I ran back to the bar to get help but didn't wait for it to get any worse. In the confusion, I slipped and fell down the exit stairwell, knocking myself unconscious. Finally, I was taken back to the hotel in an ambulance.

The next day I met Sid. The Sex Pistols were playing a gloomy venue outside of London in some college or university. Sid and I were talking on the balcony outside the dressing room, looking down over the audience in the theater.

"Sid", I said to him, as I scanned their backline on the stage below, "you guys don't have lights or a P.A. set up."

"Right, ain't it", he replied.

"Yeah, right", I answered back.

There were a few thousand people in the place. How was anyone going to see or hear them when they went on? The audience was really geared up for it and the atmosphere was party-like, but backstage it was a little depressing. Sid asked me if I wanted a beer and then went into the dressing room—from which he had been banned—to fetch one for me. He came back with the beer and it was already opened. I didn't trust this because the Ramones always put a few drops of piss in anything they gave their guests to drink after the show, as a little joke to laugh about later. I figured that the Pistols would do the same thing, so I avoided Sid's generosity. When no one was looking I poured the beer into their manager's empty glass; he drank it down in one gulp.

"I know Malcolm doesn't like me, so I am going, Sid", I said, and made my escape.

The same thing had happened the previous year when Johnny Rotten had come backstage to see us at the Roundhouse. Johnny Ramone was very friendly to him, shook his hand, patted him on the back, and asked him if he wanted a beer. Johnny Rotten took it from Johnny Ramone and then while John was smirking, he drank it down in one gulp. I was holding my breath. This is unbelievable, I thought to myself. When Johnny Rotten left, we couldn't believe that he'd come to see us.

Even though we were doing well in Europe and England, life on the road with The Ramones was not an easy way to live. I liked it in Europe, but The Ramones couldn't get used to it and started to hate going there, especially as English audiences liked to spit at us. We still kept going back to tour, but it wasn't any fun. There was a lot of tension between the band members. Johnny Ramone would yell at everybody when he came off stage. When we returned to the States, we would go back to playing places on the same level as CBGB's. You couldn't win. Sometimes it seemed like people just came to the show to hate us and to look for a fight.

The Sex Pistols were selling more records and getting more famous and The Ramones felt like they weren't getting any respect. The British press treated us like clowns. At first, we went on the defensive and acted tough.

Then, we stopped caring. The rot was setting in. After a disastrous tour of America, the Sex Pistols broke up.

Then Tommy left the Ramones. I had been watching him deteriorate on the road. Tommy didn't hold up too well—he wasn't really made of the real stuff that rock stars are made of. Then one day he was gone. I went to a band rehearsal in New York and Marc Bell was there. John and Joey had asked him to join the band. We could never recapture that classic punk sound after Tommy left, but with Marc in the band we got a very hard player. Marc had been my drinking buddy before he joined the Ramones and I loved to party with him. We both started going down the road to ruin together. The two of us spelled trouble, but to me he was more fun than John or Joey and I was glad to have him in the band.

The Ramones somehow couldn't accept him, though, and Marc realised it. We stopped getting along and drinking together because of the tension. By then, the Ramones had a no-alcohol policy that I wouldn't conform to and neither would Marc. I started arguing with Johnny Ramone because I felt the band was blaming me for all our failures. I was the most fucked up and the weakest one in the band and I was starting to hate their guts. John and Joey were laughing at how Marc was behaving and taking a real glee in instigating his hostility towards me. They started telling him little white lies, like it was *my* decision that he didn't get any money for the T shirts we sold. Stuff like that was really pissing me off.

Maybe John had the worst role in the band—as an authority fig-ure—someone had to take it. But, maybe that's what made him so un-pleasant. Or perhaps he was just doing everyone else's dirty work. In the music business it really is true, you don't get anywhere except by shout-ing, threatening, fighting, and this type of behavior. It always ends up be-ing unpleasant. You have to fight for everything. Everything. Every single aspect of your daily life—to get a show done, get on the road, get every-body to take their positions, get the money, get it done, get out of there, get the equipment out. Someone has to do it. So John had to do a lot of that, and I think it took years off his life. No one gave him any sympathy for it, all the grief he had to put up with. But he milked it for all it was

Above and below: Live at CBGB's, June 1977. (*Godlis*)

worth—I didn't see that happening. I saw that as Johnny Ramone's rules, Johnny Ramone's justifications, not mine.

One of the rules was that we had a dress code. We adopted the uniform of ripped jeans, bowl haircut, leather jackets and sneakers. It was all part of being a Ramone. Once, when we flew home from Amsterdam after a long tour of Europe, I did the opposite of what everyone thought I would do. I stayed sober on the flight back home to the States and took a good look at what was going on. Marc was as drunk as a skunk and acting insane. John and Joey, and their girlfriends Roxy and Linda, were being horrible to me.

When we cleared customs at Kennedy, I walked over to John and cursed him out. I felt like I didn't want to be a Ramone any more. To me, it was bullshit. I didn't need them to tell me what to do all the time and then rail on me. I did a lot for them. I had put my life into the band, but nothing could satisfy them. They ended up creating an enemy right in their own ranks—me. It was pretty damn stupid. Especially for Roxy and Linda to start up with me. I was sick of it. I was sick of the Ramones, the haircut as well. When I got home from the airport, I marched straight into the bathroom and cut my hair off into a Sid Vicious hairstyle. They won't like this, I thought, and made a Sid-like sneer into the mirror.

End Of The Century

The first time I met Phil Spector was at a club called the Whiskey A Go Go on Sunset Boulevard in Hollywood, California.

Phil was there to see Blondie who were playing that night. Somehow I got lucky enough to have a day off from touring and be in Los Angeles at the same time.

Blondie and Deborah Harry were friends of mine and were starting to have some success with a song called "Denis", which Richard Gottehrer had produced. But Phil had the idea he could do better, and I think he was obsessed with stealing Deborah Harry away from Blondie, producing a record for her and making her a major star. Perhaps he was in love with her and secretly wanted to marry her, who knows?

Blondie were really good that night, and I was having a great time. Deborah Harry was smashing, and wearing one of the shortest mini-skirts I had ever seen her wear. All the boys were crowding the front of the stage, trying to get a look up her skirt at her white bikini briefs. It was all quite enjoyable and I was making it better for myself by buying round after round of drinks for all the patrons in the club. I was already so drunk by

Backstage at the PalladiumTheater NYC, October 1977. Iggy Pop was also on the bill.
l-r: Janis Schacht (our publicist), Tommy, me, Roxy (Johnny's girlfriend),
Joey, Johnny, Seymour Stein, Linda Stein. *(Bob Gruen)*

Playing at CBGB's 1977. *(Godlis)*

the time I got to the Whiskey that when Blondie came on stage I had very little idea of what I was doing.

As excited as Los Angeles was to have Deborah Harry and Blondie finally playing in their city, I could sense that there was one sourpuss in the audience that did not appreciate what was going on. My psychic intuition was later to prove accurate, as I found out after the concert when I tried to go backstage and mingle with the band. I was stinking of rum and very tipsy. But it was no great challenge for me to find my way up the stairs to the Whiskey A Go Go's backstage dressing room, as I had been there so many times before. But, as I was walking up the stairs, my way was blocked by a man holding the red velvet curtains at the top of the staircase together so as not to let me pass through. This man I can only describe as resembling Count Dracula himself. He was dressed in a batwing-type cloak, he had a black beard and moustache which gave him a devilish appearance, and his dark aviator shades gave him an aura of menace and mystery. Later I discovered that this man was the crown prince of darkness himself, Mr Phil Spector.

"Where do you think you are going?", he addressed me.

"I'm going to see Debbie now", I told him.

"Not on your life", he told me.

But at just the right moment, a drunken and stoned Jimmy Destri opened the dressing room door and everyone spilled out towards the entrance-way past Phil, sweeping us inside. There was little he could do. Phil was furious, because a hot and sweaty Deborah Harry was sitting there in the dressing room, clad only in her bra and panties—she hadn't had time to change yet. I don't know if Phil had ever seen Debbie in this state before, but I sensed he didn't want anyone else to. So he was really pissed off and when he entered the dressing room and saw Debbie, freshening up her lipstick and being very friendly to me, he formed a instant bitter dislike to me, before he even knew me.

The name Phil Spector was mentioned to me again shortly upon my return to New York. Danny Fields informed us that Seymour Stein had decided that it would be good if the next Ramones album were to to be produced by Phil Spector. This was around the time the Ramones were involved with the "Rock'n'Roll High School" movie, 1978 or 79. I think the original idea for working with Phil was for him to produce the song "Rock'n'Roll High School" for the movie soundtrack. Maybe the record company thought that they could make a hit out of punk rock in the US by having Phil produce us.

By this time Seymour had really gone out on a limb for the Ramones. We still hadn't scored a hit, but no one was giving up on us and it made sense that perhaps a movie with music by Phil Spector and the Ramones would be a success. So Danny and Linda Stein invited me for a lunch/business conference at the Russian Tea Room on 57th Street, which is across the street from their management office and not too far from Studio 54.

My memory about dates and specific events is fuzzy. I was heavily into sedatives and prone to falling asleep at any time. It was hard to communicate with me—I had no interest in anything. I don't even remember the plane ride that brought me to Los Angeles for those fateful Ramones-Spector sessions. I may have already been in Los Angeles for a couple of months working on the "Rock'n'Roll High School" movie, which makes sense because I can imagine that Danny and Linda would have thought it best for us to do the album and movie simultaneously, to make the most productive use of our stay in Los Angeles.

I think I remember being in the Gold Star studio with the Paley Brothers, trying to record a song called "Come on, Let's Go" and I couldn't remember how to play it. I had done the simple bass part hundreds of times and each time I made a serious mistake. Maybe the Gold Star studios was just too historic a place for me. This was where Phil Spector created his Frankenstein experiments and the Beach Boys supposedly blew their minds.

In the studio there were many large hospital-type oxygen tanks, complete with face masks and valve regulators for use either as a hangover cure or to aid alertness. This was supposedly invented by Brian Wilson. Underneath the studio floor was a swimming pool which was used as an echo chamber—when Phil Spector started recording, studio techniques were still too primitive to achieve these effects normally, so he had to do things this way to get what he wanted.

I guess that's why there was an aura of underlying threat. Maybe my imagination was set off from hearing so much talk about handguns and personal bodyguards and karate techniques. Finally I finished "Come on, Let's Go", and amazingly despite the recording conditions and my immediate surroundings, the song came out quite cheerful.

Later, after I left Phil's laboratory at the Gold Star Studios, with Monte and the band, we went to meet Phil. Ed Stasium the co-producer of "End of the Century", escorted us to an out-of-the-way rehearsal studio in Hollywood somewhere. We tuned the guitar and bass and started struggling through "Rock'n'Roll High School". The stage was at the end of a big, long room with a very highly polished floor. As we were halfway through the song, Phil appeared and walked confidently to the center of the empty room, placed his briefcase in an open position, and, as there was no chair, crouched on the floor, peering at us from behind his briefcase. Needless to say, it had been a long day and I was losing my sense of humor and really feeling like I could use a good sleep. I don't know what Phil was doing behind his briefcase, but something seemed very suspicious to me about this type of behavior. When we finished playing the song, Phil walked over to us and congratulated us on how good the song sounded, but I still felt very ill-at-ease

I guess this was all just one of Phil's tests to scrutinise us before agreeing to produce us. I guess the next step was for Phil to see if he could enjoy being around us. After all we would be in each other's company for quite a long time, as it takes Phil a long time to complete an album. Everybody looked beat, probably from partying every night, so we all made a polite excuse to part our separate ways and meet again the next day at Phil's mansion in Beverly Hills.

The drive to his house was up a steep highway. When we arrived the place was like a heavily fortified mansion and we had to press a button and wait until we had cleared a security check and the roadblocks from the gateway to the house. His estate was a bit shabby and not very well kept. Maybe it was because he was a bachelor and lived there alone with his huge St Bernard and two bodyguards. As far as I could see, his only other friend at the time seemed to be disc jockey Rodney Bingenheimer. We knew Rodney as he had The Ramones on his first show for KROQ in Los Angeles in 1976.

Once inside his home, Phil took us for a brief tour. I'm a big fan of Phil Spector's music and, as out of it as I was at the time, I was aware that I was in the presence of a great rock'n'roll legend, but he was really making me nervous. After the tour of his mansion, he left me, John and Marky downstairs in the piano room, while he took Joey upstairs for a private conference. After about three hours I was getting restless, sitting there in that room with nothing to do except stare at John and Marc. Finally I got up off the couch and tried to find Phil and Joey to see what was up. Phil must have thought I was an intruder. I really don't know what provoked him, but the next thing I knew Phil appeared at the top of the staircase, shouting and waving a pistol. Then he practically field-stripped the thing in two seconds flat, put it back together in two more seconds flat. He had all the quick-draw, shoot-to-kill pistol techniques. Like Jimi Hendrix only with a pistol instead of a guitar.

"I can't believe this", I thought to myself. "I'm bored to death, I've got to get the fuck out of here".

"Phil", I challenged him, "I don't know what your fucking problem is, waving that pistol around and all that stuff, and trying to steal Joey away from the Ramones? I've had it. I'm going back to the Tropicana", which was the hotel on Santa Monica Boulevard where we were staying.

"You're not going anywhere, Dee Dee", Phil said.

He leveled his gun at my heart and then motioned for me and the rest of the band to get back in the piano room. Everybody sat down on the couch and had another beer. We were all very drunk by then—I was fed up, confused and hungry. Phil was a merciless host. He only holstered his pistol when he felt secure that his bodyguards could take over. Then he sat down at his black concert piano and made us listen to him play and sing

Me with Stiv Bators from the Dead Boys, 1977, New York.. *(Roberta Bayley)*

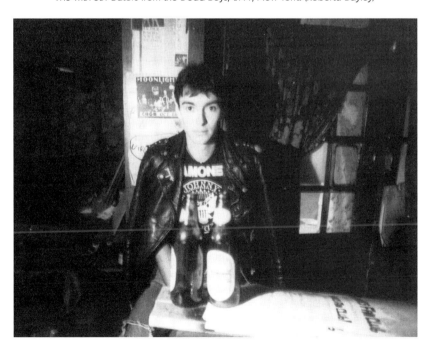

Arturo Vega sitting at the entrance to CBGB's, 1978. *(Godlis)*

"Baby I Love You" until well after 4.30 in the morning. By 5.00 a.m. I felt as if I was going to completely lose my mind.

Two weeks later Johnny Ramone, Marky Ramone, Joey, me, Ed Stasium and Phil Spector were in a studio in another secret location in Hollywood. We had been working for at least fourteen or fifteen hours a day for thirteen days straight and we still hadn't recorded one note of music. I can't imagine why, but I was getting impatient. Phil would sit in the control room and would listen through the headphones to Marky hit one note on the drum, hour after hour, after hour, after hour. It sort of reminded me of being back in Forest Hills, in Birchwood Towers with Joey Ramone in his mother's apartment, dribbling a basketball for hour after hour while Joey got it on tape.

During one lunch break a couple of days later, I asked Ed, "Where's John now?" and Ed replied "Oh, John left five hours ago. He flew back to New York."

"That's crazy", I said, "we haven't even begun recording the album."

"Well what can I tell you?" Ed told me, "I think he was trying to hide a lot of anxiety."

I went back by the soda machines and lounge area and saw Marky. "Marky" I said, "John left. He went back to New York. What do you think we should do?"

"Let's go home", Marky said.

I don't know how we did it, but somehow Marky and I managed to book a flight back home to New York that evening at seven o'clock. The next morning we were back at JFK airport. To this day I still have no idea how they made the album "End of the Century", or who actually played bass on it.

Chicken Beak Boy

When I wasn't touring with the Ramones, I went home to my little base-ment apartment in Whitestone which is a boring, middle-class neighbor-hood. I lived there ten years, but it never felt like home. My landlord lived above me and he wasn't exactly the rock 'n' roll type. I was too nervous to play my stereo, or play my bass through an amp. Everybody was just into other things like planting crummy sunflowers all around their homes. Je-sus Christ, I am more like a vampire type. It was not my kind of environ-ment.

Then, one day, my landlord's son rang my bell. I totally freaked when I saw this little kid standing out there. I felt very uncomfortable—the whole apartment smelled of pot smoke. I told him to come back later. Soon, he was at the door again and sort of vaguely communicating to me in broken English that he was interested in guitars and stuff. I went and got one of my electric guitars and gave it to him.

"Take this", I said.

I was trying to do something that my father had never done for me. I didn't know what it was like to have a kid. I've never had any, which used to bother me, but it doesn't now. My life was so shitty that it was really better that I didn't bother having a family.

Although Whitestone is a nice middle-class family neighborhood, it's a total drug neighborhood too. I could have cocaine delivered as easily as pizza. But I was mainly into smoking pot then, though. I was smoking about an ounce of it a day. It was causing me a lot of anxiety.

One of the things that I liked about visiting a place like Amsterdam was all the things you can get there legally that you can't get in the United States. In Holland you can buy cannabis legally. The menu for marijuana is written on a chalk board in coffee shops to tell you what kinds are available for the day. My favourite was Zero Zero, an opiate hash that really got me stoned.

When we played the Paradiso in Amsterdam, the hash store in the club would open after the soundcheck. I would try to buy the largest amount of hash they would sell me, and would explain myself with hand signs and signals. I'd make both my thumbs and index fingers into two zeros and go "Zero Zero" to them at the counter in a slow, careful way. Then I'd make smoking sounds at them and finally I'd make off with the Zero Zero to the hotel to smoke.

To go from that back to Whitestone was pretty grim for a pot smoker. I would try to make up for how mundane life was in Whitestone by starting my day off with six or seven joints of Buddha Thai. When I got really frustrated, I'd go to McDonalds on Francis Lewis Boulevard to cop some coke from my friend Tony Blow, the local dealer.

For a while, I had a girlfriend in England. Her name was Jill. When I first met her, she had on a red and black mohair sweater and black patent leather pants. She was very cool-looking and nice to me, but somehow I always went running back to Whitestone in terror—to be alone again. I don't know why.

The drugs and booze had taken a toll on me. They had made everything worse. My brain felt like slush. All I knew how to do was play bass in a band and be on the road. I had to tour to pay my bills. By the time the "Pleasant Dreams" album came out in 1981, I knew I'd had enough. I could see that getting high was getting me nowhere. Finally I started going to Odyssey House in the East Village as an out-patient. It was a chance for things to get better.

I was really trying hard. I knew that I was out of shape and when I got a break off the road, I started going to the gym in College Point to lift weights. No one else who went to that gym actually needed to go there but me. It was comical. I am a 90-pound weakling type—they were all real heavily built construction worker types. I was upsetting the vibes of the place. Finally someone started mouthing off to me and I got pissed off. I marched over to him and hit him in the gut. He was too big to hit any-where else. He freaked. Everybody did. The place went dead silent. We were all cracking up. They couldn't believe what they had just seen. Somehow they didn't kill me, and I got away with a humble exit and a warning, "Don't ever come back here again, you creep." I was thankful for that, but I could feel myself going a bit mental.

Outside I climbed into the brand new car I had bought on credit. It was a metallic blue Camaro with smoked chrome mags and white wall tires and a T top. Most of the cars around College Point had the standard black primer color and angry roaring tires. My car was a bit flashy for the Point and I was feeling very paranoid and edgy since I was smoking lots of pot. After the incident at the gym I decided it would be better to go to an AA meeting than take a risk going home and breaking my sobriety. So with all this mental commotion going through my head, I pulled out of my parking spot only to notice a woman pushing a baby carriage, walking right into the Camaro. I couldn't believe it. Everything went blurry and when I tried to step on the brakes I stepped on the gas pedal instead. The Camaro went berserk and I rammed it into my neighbor's van.

I got out to look at the damage. My car was fucked but I tied the hood down with some rope I had found in the garbage and I was set. I looked around to see what had happened to the woman and her baby—it didn't look like I'd hit her—so I got back in my car and somehow I backed it out of the parking space.

Then I proceeded down Bayside Boulevard to the AA meeting that was being held at some church in the area. It was so cold that when I pulled up in front of the meeting, the car doors wouldn't lock because they had frozen solid. Finally I managed to get the car locked but the keys got stuck in the lock. By then I was really fed up and thinking of just going to the store and buying a bottle of brandy, but I got a hold of myself. Fuck this, I thought. Nothing's going to bother me. I hadn't taken a car out for years and was determined to enjoy myself. I was a bit uncomfortable anyway, as I always am when I go to a meeting and smoke, but somehow I felt sober.

Just as soon as I got to the meeting, I felt that they were all against me. They could only criticize me. Finally I got up from the table and began sharing, "Hello, I am Dee Dee. I have 86 days clean." I could see them all cringing. Boy, nobody gives me any credit. I was going to say something else, but instead I stormed into the kitchen to get some cookies because I really had the munchies bad.

Eventually, the high from the joint I had smoked before the meeting fizzled out and I sneaked out of the place only to find the locks on my car had frozen again. After much banging and shouting, I got inside and behind the wheel again. But the door wouldn't shut. I stepped on the gas in frustration and as I sped around the corner the door opened again. Another car was coming directly at me, so I swerved to avoid a crash. The other car took the left side door clean off my Camaro as I scraped the paint off all the cars parked next to the sidewalk on my right. The cops took my car away. I guess they thought I was too out of control to drive.

Out of spite I went out and bought a three-quarter length car coat. Being a Ramone I was only supposed to wear leather motorcycle jackets. I guess I should have called it quits then, but I was really aggravated, so I dyed my hair blue-black and took to wearing a pair of Ray Bans as a shield between me and the rest of the world. They blocked out everything, like the dope used to. Also I switched to straight black jeans that I got from Trash and Vaudeville in the Village. I was supposed only to wear ripped blue jeans in The Ramones. The way I looked at it, at least it would stop the kids in the audience rushing the stage and grabbing the rip in my jeans and pulling it down to my ankles. I used to hate that.

John and Joey decided to lighten up on me though—at least I was trying hard not to drink and I hardly ever did coke any more. But, just as the tension between John, Joey and me started to melt so it became Marc Bell's turn in the spotlight. We had stopped touring to start work on the *Subterranean Jungle* album in New York. We were rehearsing at the Daily Planet, a studio on West 30th Street that I used to really like. Things weren't working out, though. Getting ready for *Subterranean Jungle* was a rough battle. Marc was starting to flip. The years of self-abuse were catching up with him. He had that "one way ticket on the crazy train" thing going. The last stop is always off the edge. You can't come back either.

Marc was coming to rehearsals really stoned and angry. Strangely, he almost seemed happy about his condition. You couldn't win by complaining about it. He would say that he had just been to see the doctor and that it was all band-related. He told us that the sessions he was having with the doctor were very painful and that the doctor had put him on dope. Then he would run out of the rehearsal room and laugh until he calmed down a bit and returned to the studio again for a while.

We had to be very careful around Marc, because he was prone to violence and dangerous. No one wanted any trouble from him. It was also funny seeing him giggling and making strange hiccuping noises after a row with us. Sometimes it got so bad we couldn't rehearse—Marc would drop his pants down to his ankles, stick his bare ass in the air and start to shake it. He would fold his arms into wings and start flapping them up and down, as if he were trying to fly for everyone. Finally he would peck with his nose and start running around the room in a frenzy, shouting "Chicken beak boy! Chicken beak boy!"

It was when we were recording on Long Island that Marc flipped completely. I had just walked into the studio and John and Joey were waiting for me by the door.

"Don't go in there, Dee Dee", they said.

"Ok. What's happening, dudes?", I replied.

"Go home", they told me. "It's Marc, he's flipped his wig. He's in there now doing that chicken beak boy dance. He's really out of control. It looks bad, Dee Dee."

I took the night off. I went back to Whitestone and worried about everything. When I got to the recording studio the next day it was a wreck. Every piece of furniture had been overturned. All the windows in the control booth had been broken and it smelled of vodka and cheap wine. There was a clean-up crew in the studio, trying to clear it up. Joey and Johnny were there, showing Billy Rogers, a session drummer from New York, a song they wanted to do. Marc wasn't there. I never found out what really happened. I asked Johnny Ramone when I arrived. He was glaring at me hatefully and I knew something was up.

"Let's get to work, Dee Dee", he answered, as if that was an explanation to where Marc was. I could tell that I was on John's shit list again.

"This sucks", I thought.

The next day I drove into Manhattan with Monte to pick up Joey to drive him to the studio. When Monte got out of the van to ring Joey's bell, I made my escape. I went down to 10th Street and First Avenue to cop. I met a dealer called Baby and I scored some coke off her. I didn't think the coke would hurt because I wasn't boozing.

I was wrong. It turned me into a paranoid schizophrenic. I became impossible to deal with. No one could trust me. I was trying to lie my way out of everything. In an attempt to change, I tried getting help by going to Odyssey House. I also went to a private psychiatrist. Nothing seemed to help. I was too far gone. Now they tell me that I was the most unpopular person that ever went to Odyssey House. Everybody was fed up with my lying and using drugs. My excuse was that they made me this way.

Hard Pressed

In the mid-eighties, the Ramones signed a three album deal with Beggars Banquet in England. We had just released the "Too Tough to Die" album and the label were doing everything possible to promote the band. Martin Mills, the head of Beggars Banquet, also signed The Cult. He wanted us to put out "Bonzo Goes To Bitburg". Johnny Ramone didn't like the song title and it caused a lot of problems. On our *Animal Boy* album the song is called "My Brain Is Hanging Upside Down" to please Johnny Ramone, a big Ronald Reagan fan. At least Joey and me fought for the title for the single. And for once, we won.

But for this album, Beggars Banquet went all out for a song I wrote with Dave Stewart of the Eurythmics called "Howling at the Moon". It was about marijuana. Beggars Banquet called Overland, our management office, and asked Joey and me to fly over to London to do press for the record. It sounded great—a good way to get away from Johnny and Marc for a while. But we knew that Monte would have to come to make sure we did our job and to baby-sit Joey and me. There wasn't much we could do about it. Monte had to be there. He was coming and that was that.

Monte had a wicked streak in him. We nicknamed him "The Detective" because he was such a snoop. He was determined that no one ever pull the wool over his eyes. It was really a drag. He was a mass of self-pitying frustration and no fun to be with. Marc Bell gave Monte the nickname "Lambie". Our sweet Lambie. It was to drive Monte crazy on purpose. Marc would work himself up into a frenzy in the van, making lamb noises until Monte would flip. Then the Lamb would threaten to drive us off the road and he would step on the gas. He would get the wild sheep-eyed look and a beet-red face and start shouting "We're all going to perish now, you fucking creeps. We're all going to get killed, Marc, because you wouldn't shut up. You're the Lamb, Marc! You! You! You!"

It would get extreme. Past ninety mph, the real action would start, the real yelling. The baying lamb noises at their most joyful. I didn't have any pet names for Monte. Joey just called him "asshole". To Joey, everyone was an asshole. Joey put Monte through a lot. Maybe he should go for counselling after he stops road managing. I bet Monte has a lot to get off his chest, most rock stars are difficult. You can form resentments.

I looked on the trip to England purely as a way of tasting the good life. I was hoping that we would all stick together and make everyone jealous when we got back to New York. It's ironic that I had to escape a popular rock'n'roll band to fulfil my fantasies, but I was a mass of frustration, and by then, very desperate. I wasn't fooling around this time. I wanted my drugs, booze and a "femme fatale" to go along with them. My mind was made up. No cretin road manager was going to sabotage my fun. I was going to party, party, party. No one was going to tell me what to do. I could see from the hen-pecked expression on Joey's face that he was in the same boat. Why couldn't we just admit that we needed to go crazy?

By the time we all dragged ourselves to the airport, Monte was already acting the worried manager. For my part I thought I deserved to have some fun. I was doing all this extra work for the Ramones—flying to England in February to do interviews with the creepy English press. The biggest assholes in the world. Smarty-farties, that's what we called them. So, was it any surprise that I needed to let loose? Jesus Christ, what harm was

Joey, Marky, Johnny and me at our last ever show at CBGB's in April 1979. *(Bob Gruen)*

Making a video for "We Want The Airwaves" in St. Mark's Place in 1981. During a break in filming, I hung out with some fans. This guy looked a little like Sid Vicious. *(Godlis)*

it to have a few drinks and some lines in the bathroom before a six-hour flight?

Monte came over to me before we boarded the plane and told me to watch it, that I was probably an alcoholic. "What do they want from me?", I thought. That's why I always ended up being sneaky. Because everybody was always on my case and not minding their own business. On the plane I told Monte to fuck off. That I was pissed off, that I was almost crazy already. I told him to take a good look at himself. That I'd only had one drink that morning—a double shot of Bailey's Irish Cream with a shot of rum poured into it. I only had one double Bloody Mary on the whole six-hour flight to London. I vowed to get them all back one day for what they were putting me through. For always ruining my fun. So I marched to the rest room on the plane and stayed there for twenty minutes. I knew that Monte would start to worry that I had overdosed in the toilet or something like that. It worked. Monte was soon politely knocking on the bathroom door, just as I predicted.

"Dee Dee, everything all right in there?"

I flung the door open and snarled, "Oh yeah, sure, right. I can't even take a shit in peace. See what I mean? You're an asshole. I hate you. It's because of assholes like you that I'm an alcoholic. And if I am one, then you made me one. Nobody cares about me. I am going to quit. As soon as we get back to New York, I am going to see a lawyer and I am going to sue the Ramones and everybody, so fuck you all."

Monte wasn't phased one bit. He just pushed his frizzy-top mug into my face and made a lamb noise at me. I wish I could translate it for you, it was sort of like "baaaaaaa he hey hehey hee ha ha ha." Horrible. Monte did the "ha ha ha" directly into my ear, which left me quite distressed. At 13,000 feet a person's ears are doubly sensitive, so it was a shitty thing to do. I went meekly back to my seat.

When the plane landed at Gatwick, the customs official gave Joey the usual hard time. Then they started up with me. Well, enough is enough. So I snarled, "Why don't you guys pick on the real crooks?"

"Huh?"

"You know you guys are a right bunch of assholes, aren't you?—and gimme back my passport, motherfuckers."

Either I'd put them in their place or they were just tired and wanted to go home or something. I don't really know, I am not a psychiatrist. But they stamped on my passport "All Special Privilege" and said "Welcome to England, Mr Colvin."

"May I proceed then?", I responded.

"Yes, sir."

"Ok, then. See you next time", and I went on my way. See how easy it can be if you know how to handle yourself?

There was a driver waiting to collect us and our luggage and scoot us to the Kensington Hilton, where we were staying. We always stayed there in those days because then the pubs used to close at 3 o'clock in the afternoon. The Kensington Hilton had an international bar for tourists so we could drink 24 hours around the clock. We could also order cheeseburgers and milkshakes any time of day or night, but in those days they were Wimpy's instead of McDonald's, so that sucked. As Americans, we thought it was important to retain certain standards while in the UK. The rooms in the London Kensington Hilton were a real treat—they had a booze-vending machine that shot out those little bottles like you could get on the plane.

As soon as I got to my room, I threw my luggage down and poured myself a shot of bourbon, a scotch, and then another bourbon, which I mixed with some warm Coke. Then I passed out for forty-five minutes. I was awakened by an amused Glorya Robinson from Red Eye, who handled the Ramones in England.

Glorya had been my girlfriend when I was 16, back in Forest Hills, and now she was living in England and had an English husband. Glorya was no saint herself, but even someone as hardened as her had some reservations about dealing with me. She was tough and quite ready for me.

"Dee Dee, you shit. Get up. Get up right now. I mean it. Someone wants to interview you. Get up, you lazy sod! I hate you!"

"Man, what a way to start the day", I thought to myself.

"OK, Glorya", I said, "I'm almost ready. Do you have a joint?"

She knew I'd ask that. But she didn't have one. Nobody seemed to have pot in England then. Maybe some creepy black hash, but no pot. Everybody had to get by on pints of beer, speed, and cheap whiskey. So all Glorya had was a half-empty pint of booze in her purse to see her through the afternoon, so I left her alone. That's England, I thought. What a bore. Then I rolled myself out of bed, because the interviewers were starting to bang on the door. The only reason I let them in is because I was hoping they would have a joint. They were just two typical beer-soaked journalists. The type that think they know everything, and are punk rock snobs who double-hate Americans because they are better at it than Limeys are. We know that, so we give them a lot of grief. The girl setting up the tape recorder was the snob. Her partner, a male, looked like a "poor" student from a rich British family. I broke the tension with a "Hey, guys, got any dope?" That seemed to do the trick. They actually had some.

"Yes, Dee Dee, we have some. Actually it's quite lovely."

"Is it speed?"

"Oh yes, and it's quite nice."

So they sprinkled me a few lines and soon I was feeling very sorry for myself, but also happy because I had an excuse to justify some outrageous behavior. But first I had to be interviewed.

"Dee Dee, how did the Ramones influence the Sex Pistols?"

"I don't know. Who cares? Why do you want to start trouble by asking me a question like that right at the start? You're creeps. Get out. Get out now."

So they went on to the next question.

"Dee Dee, what did you think of the British punk bands?"

I went blank. I was so confused and feeling so dishonest that I was really getting annoyed.

"Get out. Get out now" I protested. "OK, Johnny Moped was alright" came out of my mouth. "I like him and the Damned, and X-Ray Spex are alright as well."

"What is your favorite British band then, Dee Dee?", the snob inter-rupted me.

"Eddie and The Hod Rods. So fuck off mate. Get out. Get out now. I am sick of all this."

"But Dee Dee, what about the Bay City Rollers?"

"Oh, hold on a minute. Now you're talking my language. 'Saturday Night', best new wave song ever, mate. So fuck off."

"Hey, how about some more speed?"

The room seemed to take on a lime green hue to it as the short English afternoon started turning into a gloomy English evening. Speed. Crummy, crummy speed. It makes you crazy.

After a while, the snob and the student left. Then there were a whole lot more interviewers coming in and out of the room. We emptied the minibar three times in three hours and called room service for beer and Cokes. I was in top form, but very sloppy.

"Anneeeey bodieee gotta joint, ta..." Somebody promised one. "I want it. I want it now, aaaah."

Then I got bored so I suggested we go meet Martin Mills, and his pals at the Korean restaurant downstairs and ditch the journalists. I excused myself and when the coast was clear, Glorya and I sneaked into the eleva-tor and rode down to the lobby. We didn't even bother to kick everybody out of the room.

"Martin's paying", Glorya told me. "Don't worry, Dee Dee. Those journalists are just the smarty farties. Nothing anyone can really do for them. But use them for what they are."

The press people were lingering downstairs in the lobby when we got there. Somehow they had beat us downstairs. We didn't even try to pre-tend to be polite. It was too late. The war had started so we just snob-marched past them into the restaurant where Martin and his pals were waiting. I don't remember anything about dinner—I immediately passed out on my garlic steak. Nobody wanted to talk to me because I was so smelly from sleeping face down in a bunch of chopped-up garlic. I woke up alone, by myself, at six o'clock in the morning. I had nothing to smoke.

I was miserable. I wished I was back in Whitestone smoking some Thai and listening to L.I.R. Fuck this, I thought to myself.

I was paranoid from all the booze and speed, but the Kensington Hilton Hotel always has a good breakfast in the morning, a treat that I looked forward to. But, in my condition, I felt like I was walking through a minefield and stepping on low self-esteem bombs that blew apart the guilt in my brain. In short, I was killing myself.

Somehow I went for breakfast. I don't know how I made it. I could barely stand up. There was puss dripping out of my eyes and my nose was dripping blood. I went back up to my room in shame, hoping no one would see me, but the hotel had those damn computer-card keys. I ended up making so much noise trying to get into my room that I woke up Monte. It was then about seven thirty. Monte had just gone to bed. But he was glad to see me.

"Dee Dee", he said, "thank God you're here. I can't remember much of last night. I was worried anyway. You know how things can be, and... and... and..."

He had a lampshade on his head. A fluffy rabbit tail was glued to his underpants. He was still stinking drunk and his nostrils were coated with a white powder, which I could only guess to be drugs. I heard a young female voice call him back into the room. She sounded French. "Montee, Montee, Babeeeee..."

Monte excused himself like a gentleman and then slammed the door in my face. What a hypocrite, I thought. I wonder what his excuse is. Is it me? Right. What about Monte's secret behavior behind closed doors in the privacy of his hotel room? Well, I'm going to stop right now. I don't want to be the big baby of the Ramones, so I won't tell on him. All I had on my mind was to get away from Monte, and getting a couple of hours of sleep until I could call the porter and have the liquor machine in my room filled up again. Soon eleven o'clock rolled around and Glorya stumbled into my room. She was trying to maintain a professional approach, trying to be sweet. It didn't matter. I was still up. I'm a pro. The BBC, Melody Maker, New Musical Express, Sounds. It was a lot. Glorya was paranoid that I wouldn't do it. I was a wreck. When I saw Monte and Joey later, I could tell they were wrecks too. We were all pretty fucked up.

"We're losers, guys", I said. "Look at us. We're pathetic. Joey, just look at yourself, you're still as drunk as a skunk. It's only midday. Monte, it looks like you had another blackout. Do you want me to go over your antics last night? And... and... and..." I was shaking so much I couldn't continue. "Christ, I need a beer. Christ man, we all do."

Everyone was in definite agreement. Monte went over to the machine to shoot out some Cokes and scotch. He was shaking as well. I knew I had to take control, so I called room service for beer and coffee.

"Everything will be OK, guys", I said.

Glorya signed the bill "Martin Mills, Beggar's Banquet". It was a pretty heavy bill. Still, I knew I'd have to pay for it all in the end. Everybody knows that. Here today, gone tomorrow. That's how it is. We all know the score. We'd been around long enough by then to know to take what we could while we could get it. Just get these interviews over with as fast as we can—skip as many as possible. The record won't sell, anyway. Let's have some fun.

So we did the interviews quick and then went back to the Korean restaurant downstairs. Tonight was party night. Hip, hip, hooray! Right on! Party, party, party! Embassy night.

"Glorya" I said. "Cancel all the fanzines first, ok?"

I just can't handle interviews. They really suck. It's always like a confrontational situation, putting me on the defensive. Then I end up flipping out and yelling, "Get out! Get out!"

I saw Jeffrey Lee Pierce from The Gun Club flip once when we played on the bill with him in a small town somewhere in Southern France. He was being interviewed by some French smarty farties and all of a sudden he flipped. The next thing you knew he was holding his white Fender Strat over his head in the battle axe position and shouting, "Get out! Get out, you dirty French bastards and don't ever come back!"

This was much like the time I remember Johnny Ramone holding his Mosrite in the battle axe position and shouting "Get out! Get out!" at Malcom McLaren in the Whiskey A Go Go dressing room. I could go on and on. But it seems, back in the Korean restaurant, I had pulled my pants down, got up on the dinner table and tried to do the chicken beak boy dance like I had seen Marc Bell do so many times before. It was seven in the morning.

I went up to my room and had a five hour speed party to get in the right mood for the Embassy. The Embassy wasn't even that special. Girls were too hard to pick up there, then you went home by yourself. Stoned. The best thing about it was that it stayed open so late that you didn't have to go home. It would be fun, but not real fun. The fun would center around the bar and getting stoned in the bathroom.

Can you imagine trying to put me into a taxi and getting me home after a night out? It could get very, very complicated. It's easy to get stranded in London. Cabs won't pick you up. Especially if you're American and very drunk. The drivers outside the Hilton are OK. They will give you a ride, but they speed and talk too much. I guess they meet too many musicians at the hotel. At six in the morning outside the Embassy it would be nice to see them, but you won't. I was already wise to this, and I was sick of it. These guys ain't going to make my life more difficult and get away with it. No way. Something so simple as hailing a cab can be a nightmare for someone like me, though, so it's always good to have a few beer bottles with you, late night in London, to fling at the cabs. They become the enemy.

I could have had real fun, but I didn't know how. I could have gone shopping for clothes at Kensington Market, but I didn't do that until after I left the band. I could have tried to meet a girl, but I was too fucked up to care. But mostly it was about being miserable back at the hotel. That's what I remember the most—being hungover in my room. Coming down. Having nothing to do. The no fun stuff. I hated myself and the narrow world I was living in. There was no way out of it. There was nowhere else as safe to go as what was destroying me. My life felt as empty as the trail of beer cans I left behind me wherever I went.

It was catching up with me. I was heading for a breakdown. I don't know how anybody dealt with me. Everybody was becoming the enemy. I was pissed off at everybody. Everyone hated my guts. I hated touring. It was such a boring way to live that any excitement—like just getting away from the other guys for a few days—was a big kick.

It was driving me off the rails. A "you're not going to make it out alive" type of panic started gripping me. As I made my way back to the hotel in the early morning I could tell I was in trouble. It was just too obvious, like the burning sky over Berlin after a bomb raid during World War II. I could tell something horrible was going to happen, like seeing Kessie the family dachshund drowning in the Wansee in Berlin, while my drunken father just stood there and did nothing. I knew I was in trouble. It wasn't a good feeling.

I went up to my room to pack and get ready for the plane ride back to New York. I was already feeling very sorry for myself, sorry for my sins. Sorry for Kessie, my dachshund, that I had let down. The guilt was terrible.

I tried to fortify my nerves by filling a half-full Coca Cola can with bourbon. This is nice, I thought to myself, it's like cough medicine. In the taxi to Heathrow Airport, I made another one for myself to get me through getting on the plane and getting to my seat, until the bar finally opened.

When we were eventually in the air, the stewardess took my order. I ordered four little bottles of rum and two cans of Coke. She was good about it, but I do remember her laughing as she placed my drinks on the tray on the armrest.

"You're not going to be any trouble, are you sir?", she asked me.

"Oh, no" I replied. "I am just going to have these drinks and then pass out. Wake me up in New York, ok?"

I'm sure she was thinking, "Oh, alright, yank, everything seems to be in order."

As she wiggled down the aisle toward the rear of the plane, I turned my head to get a quick look at her ass. Very quickly, so as not to bring attention to myself, I twisted open one of the rum bottles and drank it in one gulp. I then twisted the other bottle open and drank that as well. I poured the other two rums into the Coke can I had just opened and drank half of it. By the time I finished the other half of the can with the rum in it, I actually did pass out for four hours.

As soon as I woke up I knew I needed a drink.

"Oh, stewardess, I need a little drink, please!"

"I'm sorry, the bar is closed. We're landing in half an hour."

"What do you mean? Just give me a quick one. It's no big deal is it? Really, I'll give you five hundred dollars! Look, here's the money!" I said, pushing a wad of dollars at her. But she backed off.

"Fasten your seat belt", she said, staring at me as she marched backwards toward the rear.

The plane had just started bucking like a maniac. It flipped her and she ended up rolling down the aisle like a bowling ball, knocking the other three stewardesses over into the passengers' seats. One busted into the toilet, breaking the door open and revealing Monte Melnick, who had been in there taking a big shitter. He was stinking drunk. He didn't know what the hell was going on.

I was glad for all the chaos, as I was going to use the diversion to steal some liquor from the drinks trolley. Somehow the plane lurched violently and bucked two or three times very severely. The third time it did so, the trolley went flying down the aisle and may well have burst through the emergency door, flown out into the cold, black sky, and fell down three thousand feet into the frozen ocean below, for all I knew or cared.

I gave up all hope right then of getting a drink. My brain was buzzing like there were hornets in my head. I was going into the DT's, withdrawing from alcohol. I really needed a drink very badly, but I knew I was not going to get one. My body started preparing to go out of control. Then they made an announcement, "Attention, we are going to circle JFK for three hours because there is a lot of winter traffic tonight and we can't get permission to land." I freaked right there in my seat. I had a breakdown. I couldn't believe what I had just heard. I really could have used some thorazine.

After an hour I was really in bad shape. The plane was shaking up and down, hitting air pockets and diving, then doing straight up climbs to avoid disaster. It kept going round and round in circles. I was contemplating suicide. I thought about jumping out of the emergency exit in a parachute. Somehow, I was trying to hide my breakdown from the other passengers and the stewardesses, but I think they could tell. Everything was coming apart at the seams.

"NNNNooooo!!!!!" I screamed over and over in my head, as they announced that we were flying over to the Hartford, Connecticut airport to land and refuel, and wait for permission to fly back to JFK to land.

"NNNNooooo!!!!! NNNNooooo!!!!! Not me!! Please!! No, this can't be happening to me!!"

"Ladies and gentlemen", they announced a second time, "we are now flying to Hartford. Please fasten your seat belts."

"NNNNooooo!!!!! Not me!!!" I had been rummaging around behind the pillows in my seat and in the pocket in front of me, where people normally put their empty bottles of booze on the trans-Atlantic flights. I was looking for a bottle with a few last drops of booze left in it. All I found was the aluminium flap from one of the Coke cans. I twirled it around in my hand between my finger and thumb. It felt sharp. I wondered if I could go into the bathroom and use it like a razor blade to cut my wrists and finish my miserable life once and for all.

I started dreaming that if we would just land I could get to one of those Korean grocery stores on Third Avenue and get a six-pack of beer, but soon I was forgetting that idea. The thought of getting anything more to drink didn't seem to be a possibility any more. What mattered most was to hold on to my sanity. I was going over and over my explanations and excuses in case I flipped out.

Psycho Therapy

When I got home to Whitestone—the plane had eventually landed in Newark, New Jersey, instead of JFK Airport—I was really in a bad way. I was convinced I was hearing classical music. I turned the stereo on and off. No, it wasn't coming from the stereo. I listened to the phone. No, not the phone. The TV set? No, there was no sound coming from the TV. I checked everything. In my craziness, I listened to the electric socket to see if "they" were broadcasting. I couldn't find where the music was coming from. It got louder and louder.

I decided to try to take a hot bath to calm myself down. When I sat in the water, it started getting real wavy. It was weird, like sitting in the ocean, not a bathtub. I had closed the glass shower doors around the bathtub to keep the steam in. Then, all of a sudden, the glass doors exploded and the glass shattered in hundreds of tiny jagged pieces. It was freaky. Whatever force it was that broke those shower doors, it wasn't subtle. The explosion was wicked, but none of the glass stuck into me or cut me. Why, I don't know, but I still got the point. Glass had filled up the bottom of the bathtub like sand in the bottom of a bucket.

I jumped right out of the bathtub. I knew that this was a message to me from the underworld, a greeting from hell. I was really paranoid by now. Twenty minutes later I was on the phone, "Hello, this is Dee Dee Ramone. I am going crazy. Send an ambulance. I am flipping out beyond return. I mean it! No-hope crazy, ok? Berserk, completely insane!"

But after I had called 911, I called Tony Blow, my coke dealer. "Hello, Tony, it's Dee Dee. Can you deliver right away? It's urgent." He came over and I got some coke from him and snorted it up. I did it as fast as humanly possible, since I was so used to doing it on the sneak anyway. Then all of a sudden the police and para-medics walked into my living room out of nowhere. Christ, I thought, I'm busted. But the detective was cheerful. I was stunned.

"Dee Dee, my friend", he said, "How would you like to go downtown?" This was about the fifth time that I had been taken away.

I didn't know what to think, but as I put two and two together, I figured that this might be my ride out of Whitestone. I needed to get to the city again to cop some more cocaine. I was coming apart at the seams. All I could think of was more coke, more coke, more coke...

"Detective, sir", I said, trying to seem cheerful, "Do you think we could swing by the East Village for a minute?"

"Why not, Dee Dee?", the detective said. "That's a great idea."

It's a miracle, I thought.

"I am ready now, let's go!" I said to him, and we headed out the door to the police van.

I started going over a plan. As soon as we got near 10th Street in the East Village, I would jump out of the van and escape. I figured I could get the jump on the cop until he pulled over and ran after me. I planned to get to Baby, cop the blow and do it all in one toot, so the police couldn't take it away. I knew already that they would catch me again right away, but what could I do? I was doing my best.

The cop was tricky, though. He got the jump on me faster than normal. He was actually in the process of kidnapping me. Going to the East Village to 10th Street and all that was just a diversionary tactic that the cop was getting me to play up to, so that I would be more manageable. In fact, the detective was actually trying to be nice about everything and get me to hospital before I flipped out completely. He had alerted the staff at Gracie Square that he was bringing me in, so everybody was waiting on the street for me.

I can usually find my way around in Manhattan, but this time I was so stoned that I didn't know where I was. I was flipping. I had had about as much as I could take. I panicked, and in my confused state, I suddenly flung open the door on my side of the van and ran like a wild man down the sidewalk.

The thing is, though, that I wasn't downtown, I was right in front of Gracie Square, and Dr Finkel, who had taken over my case from Dr Hanch at Odyssey House, was there waiting for them to bring me in. He spotted me immediately. He was obviously expecting me to be difficult and had his personal hospital assistants positioned strategically on the block. They caught me fairly easily—I was very out of shape and near a complete breakdown by then. They put me in a restraining device and gave me a massive dose of thorazine to calm me down. After they wrestled me into the building and into the elevator, Dr Finkel took out his stethoscope and notepad and looked me over. After three minutes, the required legal minimum for observation, he declared me totally insane and put me in the quiet room for the night.

All I can remember about the rest of what happened is that I woke up the next day in the rubber room in Gracie Square, a well-known institution in New York. It was sort of like that place in the Ramones "Psycho Therapy" video. It was real scary. I am used to the worst, but this was the absolute pits. Being surrounded by a bunch of maniacs was too much for me. I started feeling very confused and sorry for myself. I had no idea where I was, if it was Manhattan, Queens, or even California. I knew I was locked up, but not in jail. I was in some kind of a deep fog.

The rubber room. It was insane. I was freaking out at first, but then I sunk into a hopeless valley of depression and went blank. Everybody had a green gown with slippers which had that yellow happy face on them. I

Me and a friend in the photo studio, October 1992. *(Bob Gruen)*

guess when you're nodding from the thorazine and your head begins to fall, you were supposed to see that face and cheer up. I had that same vacant look on my face like everyone else did, and we were all looking at each other.

When trouble started, it was usually because someone was looking at someone else the wrong way. To this day I flip if someone looks at me the wrong way. Finally, I started coming down and they put me in amongst the regular population. I was given a room to share with a negro. He was quiet and well-behaved. He just lay on his cot, sleeping with his eyes open, and I sat in the window frame looking at a light bulb.

I was snapping out of it, but then they moved a Spanish guy in on us who was a crack addict with shredded lungs. He would twist and turn all night. His teeth would be chattering and his lungs wheezing. Finally he would pass out for an hour or two and start snoring. The noise became so threatening and disturbing that Dr Finkel decided to put me in a room with some guys who were less hopelessly damaged and more settled into the hospital. The idea was that I could pull myself together and settle my nerves. They put me in with a huge black guy called Tree Top and an overweight, swishy Spanish queen. Tree Top was as strong as an oak, but a good person and not violent at all. The queen drove me berserk. He talked all day long about his oversexed mother and his childhood in the Bronx, and about a place he used to go called the Indian Rock.

I was the oldest one there, the only dope fiend and the only one who had never done crack. I couldn't relate to this new breed of addicts. It was spooky. Can you imagine how Tree Top and that queen were pushing my buttons? They were in great spirits and delighted to have me there. They were planning our future together and were determined that we would hang out together when they let us go. The queen wanted to take me to some park in the Bronx to show me the Indian Rock. I was flipping. I hadn't had any sleep for five days. They made me go to classes and AA meetings all day, and then put me in a dual focus group. I had to do something, so I started hiding in the space between my bed and the wall, so no-one could find me and I wouldn't have to go anywhere.

Tree Top was a little stupid, though, and he wouldn't leave the room unless I would go with him. Finally I would just hop into the crack between my bed and the wall. Tree Top would start losing it then. His eyes would get wilder and more paranoid by the second. Anybody could tell that I was hiding where I was, because he was making it so obvious that something was up. When Dr Finkel came into the room to see what was going on, he would shout, "Tree Top, where's Douglas?" and Tree Top would point to where I was and say, "He's there." That was fucked up. They also made me play volleyball. It was a nightmare.

Finally, Tree Top's snoring and the queens's babbling drove me over the edge. It was the fifth day, four in the morning, and I had finally gone insane. I overturned a trash can and started banging it with a Coca Cola can.

"Good morning, motherfuckers! Good morning, fucking asshole creeps. Good morning, did you hear me? I am getting the hell out of here! You guys have driven me berserk. Are you happy now?"

Then I froze. The hurt look on the queen's ugly mug was so sorrowful. Tree Top was terrified and hiding between his bed and the space between the wall. I've seen it all, I thought to myself. I can't take any more of this. I just shut up. The vibes were terrible. We were all drained. I grabbed a shopping bag and a black plastic Hefty bag and started packing up my stuff.

"Bye, bye, assholes!", I shouted, and then started struggling out the door and into the hallway.

"Where you going?" Tree Top hollered. I was stalling anyway, so I took advantage of the grace of the moment.

"I'm gettin' outta here! I'm going!"

"Oh, Dee Dee, darling!", the queen said, daring me to make one more move. "If you make a fuss around here, they'll put you in a restraining device and throw you in the rubber room."

"Even if I just wanna leave?" I said, feeling a bit defeated.

"Jesus Christ!" Tree Top said. "You can't just leave here when you want to, man! This is a mental institution! You lost all human rights when they locked you in this joint. So shut the fuck up!"

"No way. I'm going."

I was real shaky, though, and I didn't want to go back to the rubber room. I felt myself coming apart at the seams again, and then Dr Finkel walked into the room. He had been working around the clock for five days straight, and hadn't been home yet, and hadn't shaved for five days. I checked his beard out and thought to myself, "he looks like a Marxist revolutionary". I calmed down right away, and decided not to shave any more either. That will drive them crazy, I thought. Even Johnny Ramone told me once that the ultimate was to shave your head and grow a beard. Which, by the way, I have done.

While I was digesting all this information, Tree Top and the queen were holding their breath. I was going blank and Dr Finkel was about to lose his cool, so I broke the ice.

"We're not doing nothing!"

"Well, what's all the commotion about, Douglas?"

"Oh, nothing."

"Well then, you guys get some sleep now! Tomorrow is going to be a long day."

They let me out of there two weeks later. When I walked back into my apartment in Whitestone I had a beard. The beard really flipped everyone out. Johnny Ramone was really against it. For the next five years I fought for my right to have a beard. I used the fact that every one of my psychiatrists had one. Sometimes I'd give in and shave it off. Then I'd grow another one. I made myself a promise some day I would be able to do as I wanted. Like Fidel Castro, Dr Finkel, the guys in ZZ Top, or the guy on the rolling paper I use to smoke marijuana. I saw a beard as the reward you earn by being a successful outlaw type like me. It means, "Stay away, don't fuck with me. I am mean. Get off my case, motherfuckers."

Los Ramones

By the time the Ramones were touring South America, the last thing I needed was any more cocaine in my system, but I was greedy and that's where the stuff comes from. When we finally landed in Buenos Aires, which was the last city on this particular tour, I was really ill. I was crashing and very demoralised. After I made it through customs, I wandered off from the band, who were making small talk with the local groupies. I had tried to get marijuana in every city in South America, but never had any luck. It was hard to get. I was freaking out by the time I got to Argentina, so I sneaked away from everyone to try to score some weed somewhere in the airport. I chanced upon a Latin American gentleman who said he could help me. We went to the parking lot together, and he had weed in the trunk of his car. It was a fancy car—he was obviously some kind of successful survivor-type.

So we hit it off. I got into his car and he drove me to the hotel. He said he could have all the cocaine he wanted, but he wasn't interested. He had lived in the jungle with the Indians on a coca paste camp. He said that he was smoking massive amounts of cocaine a day before he hit bottom.

Then he had to pull himself slowly back to sanity. He said that the drugs really did a number on him—that with drugs, you couldn't win.

"Dee Dee", he told me, "It is common knowledge that Che Guevara ran dope into the United States to fuck up American society."

Whenever I toured South America with the Ramones, I came home a mess. Before I left I always had high hopes that it would be the "Big One." In Whitestone, about the most excitement I got was watching the girls in the ZZ Top videos on MTV. I was eager to get to Rio, the city that boasts the world's most beautiful women. Everyone else felt the same way, but we were also trying to keep our home lives calm. When Monte came to pick me up, I tried to act miserable, and said a meek goodbye to Mr Smith, my pet parrot, so as not to upset him. Monte scooted me out the door and into the van. As soon as we were on the Brooklyn-Queens Expressway, I let out a "Hip Hip Hooray!" and lit up a joint. I was dreaming about topless beaches, girls and cocaine.

"Forget it, Dee Dee", Monte said. He could see trouble. "We're only going to Sao Paolo and Buenos Aires. Rio is too much of a party town. So, I told the promoter not to book us there."

I couldn't believe him. Monte seemed like he might get really difficult this time. I tried to play innocent to keep him level. After all, he was driving. He had threatened to drive the van off the road in the past when he was stressed, and I believed that one day he would actually do it. I just wanted to be partying in South America, far away from Whitestone.

When we got to the airport, I saw Joey and everybody standing around waiting to board the plane. You could tell right away that they were trying to hide something, trying to look inconspicuous, but it was an act. I was acting as well. We were trying to keep up a professional front, but flashed each other secret smirks, suggesting sin and debauchery, to keep up our courage. Everybody played the game and behaved themselves on the flight. We cleared customs with no trouble, then we went to our rooms in the hotel in Sao Paolo and there was nothing to do. I was full of anxiety, but I thought, this place isn't so bad.

I had previously placed my order for cocaine, and someone was supposed to score for me while I waited in my room at the hotel for them. They were taking their sweet time and I had had enough. I was about to flip.

"Motherfuckers! Cocksuckers! I hate everybody's guts! Are you happy now? Is this what you want?"

I had been there five hours already, and all I was getting was the old runaround. I never felt so mean in my life Here was my one chance to do cocaine in South America, and life plays another sick joke on me. I've heard from everyone I asked that everybody has it. It's excellent. You can get it everywhere, that it's 10 dollars a gram, the purest rocks around. Well, why don't I have any then? Typical. They didn't get us any marijuana either. It was a nightmare. I waited up all night for the phone to ring, but no one called or came by my room. Finally we let a fan come backstage after our show. Normally we wouldn't do that, but I was desperate. I had to sit there and make small talk with him while he took forever to roll a spliff, which was ninety percent rolling paper, tobacco, and such a small piece of black hash that I didn't even get a buzz.

I was hoping for a party when we got back to the hotel, and I wasn't disappointed. It was pretty lively. The show had been a big success, and there was a bunch of hot Latin babes prowling around in the shortest miniskirts I have ever seen. They were offering themselves to us and trying to get in the elevator with us to come to our rooms.

At the bar in the lobby of the hotel, the elite of the Brazilian underground night creatures were hanging out and waiting for us. The hotel guests were hanging out at the bar and in the lobby, and everyone was real, real stoned. There was no pretense of being goody-goody types. That went out the window right away. It was great. What a night!

They had a doctor to dispense cocaine to the lucky few. It was supposed to be the ultimate to get coke from him. He had a little black medicine bag and a white doctor's uniform on. He made us all feel better. I was having the time of my life, riding the elevators up and down and making faces at people, running up and down the halls, yelling.

My little folly turned sour around eight in the morning in the hotel lobby coffee shop. I was sitting there alone, very demoralised and crashing. I ordered a few beers and tried to eat breakfast, to try and pull myself together, but my hangover was starting to overpower me, and I still had to pack my suitcase, I had a flight to catch in an hour...

Heart Of Poison

When we got back to New York, there were a lot of rumors flying around. Everyone was in trouble. We went right into the studio to work on the *Animal Boy* album, and there was more commotion than usual. Matt Lolya, one of the road crew, showed up at the studio with his stuff in a black plastic Hefty bag and a shopping bag from some supermarket in Brooklyn. His old lady had thrown him out. It was a strange way to record an album.

When we were laying down the tracks for a song called "Love Kills" about Sid Vicious, I was so nervous that I couldn't play the bass part and John had to do it. I excused myself and went to the bathroom and poured myself a drink from the bottle of wine that I had hidden between the trash can and the plastic liner bag. Then I went back into the studio to argue with everybody, but by then it didn't matter. I was having severe chest pains, so we had to end early.

"This ain't so bad", I thought to myself. Since we'd ended early, I figured I could sneak over to 10th Street to see Baby and cop some coke. I decided I would go to see my doctor the next day about the pains in my chest. If I was going to have a heart attack, there was no way I was going to sing "Wart Hog" when we played New Haven the next day. They made me sing it anyway. I tried to stick up for myself, but The Ramones are very stubborn—they always won.

Except for once, somewhere in the Catskills at a Jewish resort in up-state New York, when I decided to get sneaky on them and play the help-less heart attack schtick that I had learned from the "Sanford and Son" show on TV. I started moaning and shifting about in the back of the van, like I imagined Fred Sanford would have done.

I started up with them, claiming that they were driving me to an early grave. I started whining that I would have a heart attack if I had to sing "Wart Hog" again. Eventually I wore them out, and they agreed to work out a deal with me to keep the peace. I still wasn't satisfied and kept up my spiel until I was in a frenzy. I insisted that Monte pull over and dial 911 and get me an ambulance. Finally, Monte pulled over and flagged down a cop car. I jumped out of the van and started running for my life. Because of my weak heart, the cops caught me pretty easily, and I spent the night under observation. I hate strange hospitals and would rather have sung "Wart Hog", but I had gone too far again. And, as usual, I had to pay the price.

By this stage, Johnny Ramone decided everything for the Ramones. I sat in the back of van and they sat up front. No one ever spoke to me. John and Joey had a few phoney conversations, but that was about it. I don't know if everyone wanted to listen to the baseball game all day, but Monte would never turn it off because John wanted it that way.

By 1985 I was starting to have more imaginary heart attacks. But in-stead of going to a psychiatrist, I insisted on going to every cardiologist in Queens and Long Island. They put me in a long tube and took X-rays of me. It was like a Frankenstein experiment; I loved it and it made me feel very special. Usually I would wake up at six o'clock in the morning, hold my heart and call the paramedics. They didn't have any sympathy for me, however, so I would just get up.

It was my favorite time of day. I would put on a strong cup of coffee, roll up six or seven joints of Buddha Thai and I'd dream myself out of

Above: Playing the Camden
Underworld, June 1994
*(Miyuki Maloney
UK Ramones Fan Club)*

Left: The Pinhead
Astoria, London, 1995
(Alan Giff, UK Ramones Fan Club)

Whitestone. By then I was having a lot of escape fantasies about jobs I could do to support myself, so I could quit the Ramones. Like being a doorman, or a candy store owner, or having a hot dog stand. I was serious. I'd had enough.

One of the best Ramones escape fantasies I had was around this time. The band was driving home from Boston. It was about six in the morning and we got to one of those toll booths in Connecticut. All the delivery trucks were lined up along the highway. The orange sun was warming up the oil and gasoline on the concrete. It all seemed very glorious to me. There were the trucks that delivered the morning papers to Queens. Then there were the bread and milk trucks that delivered to little grocery stores. It all seemed so friendly.

I've been driving this route between Boston and New York for seventeen years now, I thought, as I took another deep drag of Thai weed. The Thai was really strong and helped me escape into a deep fantasy—I was going to buy a Wonder Bread delivery truck to take bread to supermarkets in Queens. Suffice to say, I just kept playing bass for the "brudders". It was real crummy.

What happened next was awful. I accepted a line of cocaine in the bathroom of the Whitestone Church at an AA meeting. Then I ended up sneaking over to Francis Lewis Boulevard to cop a gram of coke from Tony Blow. That really set me back. For about six months I became cocaine crazy.

Alligator Alley

When I got into rap I didn't exactly win any popularity contests. After I showed up for the video shoot for "I Wanna Live" in a rap outfit that I'd bought at Doctor Jay's in Flushing. A maroon WHAT? jumpsuit, gold chains and a kangol. The rest of the band hit the ceiling. We drove to a studio in New Jersey to try to shoot the video. If they had had it with me at this point, then fine. I'd sure had it with them. I had a real bad hangover and felt suicidal. It's funny that I was going to do a video for a song called "I Wanna Live". I wanted to die.

Marc Bell came to my rescue. He still saw some worth in me as a songwriter for the band, and was worried about his future. He had bills to pay. That's normal. It was also his turn to keep it together. Marc tried the good bunny approach.

"Good little bunny" he remarked. "How's my little bunny today? Stop complaining, and don't worry Dee Dee. You're loved."

"I am?", I said, getting all starry-eyed and falling for it.

"Remember, Dee Dee", said Marc, "the good bunny gets the carrot. Carrots are good. Remember, we are bunny men and we need our carrots."

I walked out of the video shoot with him, me trailing slightly behind Marc. He was trying to keep me calm, then, before I knew what happened, he grabbed my arm and twisted it behind my back. Marc is a big strong guy. There was nothing I could do. He snatched my 007 out of my sock and with his free hand he took the eight-ball that was stashed under my kangol.

The video director had had it with me, though. He wanted to sue me. The whole thing got so complex. I don't really know what I had done that was so serious. I had to sign a paper for everybody to stay out of court. Then we got on a small plane and flew to Atlanta to play a show so they could get live footage for the video. They also had us playing a show in New York at a club called the Ritz, which I couldn't make it because I was so nervous.

Marc Bell saved the day, I guess. He had a couple of friends from Brooklyn that he sometimes associated with. They were very much like the types in "The Honeymooners", the old TV show starring Jackie Gleason. One of the cool things about Marc is the Brooklyn in him. It's his toughness and his sweetness. It makes him seem out of place in somewhere like Florida. But, we were playing a lot of shows down south and heading from Georgia through Alabama toward Florida, driving down the highway in our Ramones van with Monte behind the wheel. The usual deal for us. We were all pretty cheerful, and expecting that "I Wanna Live" would be a big hit, and that they were gonna play it on MTV every day—we were already counting the money. We pulled over to a Stucky's gas station and peanut store, and there was Zippy, a friend of Marc's from Brooklyn. Zippy was gassing up his car. His car seemed pretty comfy, and the Ramones van seemed very stuffy, so we asked Zippy:

"Where you going, dude?"

"Florida, my friends, Florida. Miami, Florida, to be exact. Yes, yes, yes, my friends, even Zippy gets a little vacation sometimes."

"Can we come?", Marc and I asked. "We're playing Miami tonight. It would be cool to hang out. Three guys from New York in Florida—pretty hot, dudes! Let's go!"

Monte was pretty pissed off. I think Joey was glad to see us go, so Marc and I got in the car with Zippy and we headed down toward the sun and fun and Miami beach. All our antennas were up and we were thriving.

The gossip was getting hot after about an hour. Zippy had all kinds of health problems since we had last seen him. I had a million questions to ask him about liver repair and liver damage. We were all wondering about guns, as you could buy them over the counter in Florida. Along the way, people were selling fire crackers and peaches by the road.

It was cool, but soon I began to notice that there were only weeds along the highway. For a long time we seemed to be driving through a swamp. Alligators were peeking at us from the bush, and I saw a snake crawl across the road real fast as we drove by. Zippy tried to run over it, and instead ran the car off the road. We were out of gas anyway, so I don't know if anything could have helped us.

As soon as the car careered off the highway, the weeds all around us caught fire from the heat of the exhaust pipes under the car. The weeds were very dry from the summer heat. The swamp is known as Alligator Alley, hundreds and hundreds of miles of wilderness that runs along one of the highways to Miami. It is not exactly a pleasant place to get stranded.We jumped out of the car and seconds later it burst into flames and started to sink slowly into what seemed like a quicksand pit.

Marc had promised Monte that he would take care of me, and that we would make the show, so he was beside himself. We were all sort of enjoying it, but I was pretty paranoid. The alligators were all flopping and spinning on the highway, where we were all huddled together to escape the flames. I was scared shitless of them, with their beady eyes and their sharp teeth. Stay away, OK? The last thing I wanted was to die in Alligator Alley along the highway in Florida. It was insane. Miles of swamp caught fire and burned completely. Later that night, we saw it on TV at the Miami Holiday Inn. I was worried about the police catching up with us, but nothing ever happened.

We had made it to the show in the back of a pick-up truck which Marc eventually flagged down by waving some hundred dollar bills at a Good

Samaritan. An old pick-up truck stopped and drove us to the theater in Miami. We gave the guy three hundred dollars. The fans were lined up on the street to see the Ramones and they couldn't believe it was Marc and me.

"Are you guys the Ramones?"

"Yeah. Excuse us, we have to get inside to do a soundcheck", we said as we darted through the stage door. Zippy was carrying the pinhead sign which he had somehow saved from the fire in the swamp. It was the same one that The Ramones used to the end. Poor Zippy.

Happy Families

However much I tried to hide my feelings, I knew pretty much I couldn't take it any more. It was explained to me that the Ramones was my job—I had to do my job. But I felt let down, like I had to do all the work. I hated it. They expected me to write one song after another, and then have ten people never say thank you. All they gave me was attitude.

One of our drummers, Richie Beau, was a good songwriter. He wrote "Somebody Put Something In My Drink". Joey is a good songwriter. He wrote "Sheena Is A Punk Rocker", "Beat On The Brat", "Judy Is A Punk" and "I Don't Care". Together we wrote "Glad To See You Go"—he put music to my lyrics. Later he wrote "I Wanna Be Sedated", "Rock'n'Roll Radio" and a lot of other great Ramones songs. The whole band wrote "Pinhead", Tommy too. Later with songs like "Psycho Therapy", I was trying to get Johnny Ramone to be less cranky, to get him in a better mood. So I would try to motivate him to get in on songwriting situations, and not just give him songs. Johnny Ramone gets a co-writing credit for "Psychotherapy" but I wrote that. I could go on and on.

It was a little absurd. I knew Joey and me were pretty helpless. We needed a lot of dedicated watching and baby-sitting. But too much control was in the hands of the music business people, management and the record company. Johnny was making too many musical decisions for a person who wasn't a songwriter. I wish he had been the one writing the songs. Nothing would have made me happier. He should have had the relationship with the management that I had to put up with. That was like living in hell. When you are on tour, having the management call you every day at 6 in the morning, asking if you have a new song when you're just trying to get to bed. Someone else in the band has been in your room for 4 hours on coke telling you he's going to quit because he's so miserable, and you've got so many bills and you don't want to write another song—you just hope that someone else in the band will write too. It got on my nerves. Johnny just criticised everything. It seemed to be his way of having fun.

It was tough recording the "Brain Drain" album because everyone took their shit out on me. I dreaded being around them. It drove me away—I didn't even end up playing on the album. Everybody in the band had problems; girlfriend problems, money problems, mental problems. It's not easy to be in the same rock'n' roll band with the same people for as long a time as the Ramones were. It just amazed me that people could keep believing in that happy family image of The Ramones. But then, I was amazed when Ricky Nelson died a drug addict. I couldn't believe it. I thought he was such a nice guy, nice songs, he was like an all-American guy. Also, when Del Shannon shot himself, it made me think of why I wanted to shoot myself too.

Somehow we loved each other though. I was staying in the band because I was so helpless and confused, but also because I was worried about them. How they felt. If they were happy, stuff like that. I worried especially about Joey.

I took a lot of abuse for being a Ramone. Once, I arrived at a New York airport with Monte, and the rest of the Ramones were already waiting. They all looked really uptight. I walked up to Johnny and said:

"John, what's goin' on?"

John answered, "I hate him", referring to Joey.

He looked pretty scary, his eyes looked like those of a killer, and he was enraged. Then he scowled at me:

"I am not going to Toronto, Dee Dee. I hate him. He used the name Ramone to play the Ritz.", referring to a solo gig Joey had played.

"It was a party, John. Joey needs another outlet, it's not..."

John cut me off:

"No way! No way! It's all or nothing! Fuck everybody. I quit! I don't need this shit!"

"Well, should I go see what Joey thinks?"

"Fuckin' go ahead!", John shot back at me.

So I walked up to Joey, who was glaring at me and John from across the room. He was obviously not going to give an inch.

"Joey, my man. How are you today?", I said.

"Fuck you, Dee Dee, you're John's friend. I am not going to Toronto today, ok? So fuck all of you."

"Now Joe bro', my man. Remember, sweet lovable all-important one, good bunnies get the carrots. Sweet bunnies with fluffy ears and tails. We are rabbits. Rabbits can't get jobs, Joey. Let's get on the plane. There are places to go and pleasures to enjoy. It's a beautiful day! What are ya worried about?"

Finally, Johnny Ramone ended up yelling at me in Gary Kurfirst's office one more time. Fuck this, I thought to myself. No more! Why couldn't Monte have crashed the van and gotten us all killed? It seemed like I spent most of my life on the pavement, so it would have been perfect to die on the highway, but that would have been too easy.

If the van had crashed we all probably would have survived, except for Monte. That would have been hilarious. I could just see our sweet Monte going through the windshield. Somehow his head would get chopped off. All our eyes would start sparkling. Johnny Ramone would be thrilled. He would flash us a "how could something this wonderful happen to us" grin, and we would all agree. The air would seem like it had twice as much oxygen, and we would gather around the van and stare at Monte's headless body like a bunch of evil bats. Someone would say:

"I've finally seen some justice in my lifetime."

Marky would be dancing around with glee, chuckling "Chicken beak boy! Chicken beak boy!"

Joey would just stand there, twirling a lock of his hair, muttering "Fuck you, Monte... Fuck you, Monte..."

Johnny Ramone would be pleased as if it were Christmas and there was a Christmas tree with nothing but presents for himself under it.

Down And Out

One of the last van rides I took with my "brudders" was on our 1989 US tour, in California. It was one of my many breaking points with them. I was seriously ill at that point. I couldn't stop throwing up. You couldn't tell how skinny I was because I was on Stellazine, Buzzbar and Trofennial. I was on large doses of these anti-depressants to take the edge off being sober. Like Marc and John, I had been sober for a few years by then. Joey was drinking like a fish and causing a lot of trouble, which Marc and John seemed to ignore.

I was convinced that they were trying to force me out of the band. Maybe they sensed that their touring days were numbered. I don't really know why. It seemed to me that they were being unbelievably cruel. I was trying to ignore it, but it hurt. Every time I threw up there would be some sort of mock concern—nobody seemed to realise that being anorexic is so humiliating. How can you talk about that with people who hate you? Anyway, I didn't ask for any favors from them because I knew I wouldn't get any. Even from Monte, who was like a nursemaid to Joey by then, and a slave to the whims of Johnny Ramone.

We traveled all over California on that tour, listening to the baseball on the radio all the time. Finally, at one point, I popped a Reba McIntyre cassette into the deck. I wanted to hear the track "Cathy's Clown", but they popped it right out of the deck.

"Forget it, Dee Dee", they said. Well, I guess I was used to it and didn't say anything—they wouldn't listen to my Motorhead tapes either when I first discovered them. Most of the time I would just sit at the back of the van staring out of the window.

By the time we got to San Francisco, we had a day off. I had finally kicked the anti-depressants, so I was feeling very ill. But Monte wouldn't take me to the hospital because Johnny and Joey wanted to go shopping for old movie posters, which they both collect for a hobby.

I was really sick, so I got in a cab and found a clinic and went in for a check-up. The doctor told me that from not eating and from being anorexic, I had a dead battery. It was suggested to me that I couldn't go on like this, and that I might have as little as three weeks to live.

In a band, on tour, if you're sick, you're sick, but the show must go on. So I finished the tour. The last show I did with them was in Santa Clara, California. Murphy's Law were opening for the Ramones. They were great, but there was some trouble, and Jimmy Gestapo threatened to kick Johnny Ramone's ass. I don't know what the problem was. Then Jimmy said that John would never be safe in New York. I wondered if that meant the rest of the Ramones as well. I was worried.

So, I bailed out. Like Reba sang in "Cathy's Clown", "a man shouldn't crawl..." Fuck it, I thought, I can make my life better than this. I want a little more than this crap I get all the time for being Dee Dee Ramone. I felt like I had paid enough dues to the whole damn system and I knew I was man enough to get out of it. After the flight back to New York, I went home to Whitestone, packed a small bag and left, never to return.

Back To The Village

The only thing left to do was to walk out on it and go back to my roots. So I moved back to Manhattan and got an apartment on 10th Street in the East Village. I put my guitar, my records and a mattress up there.

This was 1989, and everything in the East Village was still like it used to be. The whole atmosphere reeked of drugs. I was shocked at how bad everyone had ended up—Stiv Bators, Richard Hell, Johnny Thunders, Cheetah Chrome. All my friends had no career and were broke, homeless or hustling on the street for drugs. You don't get any sympathy when you're a down and out rock star.

Back in Manhattan, I felt kind of edgy. I could hear all the noises on the street from my apartment window, which had a nice view of one of the top dope spots. The city looked weird to me, but I soon got the courage up to scramble down the stairs and hit the street.

Walking between First and Second Avenues, you have to walk through a maze of dope dealers and addicts. I scooted past them to Second and St Mark's Place, and then walked up to Third Avenue, where I ran into Johnny Thunders by the Continental Divide. He looked bad. He was shak-

Above left: Me and Banfield the dog, New York, 1997. *(Veronica Kofman)*
Above right: A hat and a Hollywood smile. Los Angeles, 1997. *(Barbara Zampini)*

Above left: Playing bass at Joey Ramone's birthday party, May 19th 1997 *(Veronica Kofman)*
Above right: Me and Barbara on St Mark's Place, NYC, outside the building where the AA
meetings were held. August 1996. *(Veronica Kofman)*

ing and obviously needed a fix. We started talking and John asked me if I wanted to go to where he was staying at a friend's place.

His friend lived at Astor Place, which was nearby. Johnny went right into the bathroom and shot up some cocaine. His friend's apartment was pretty nice and I was glad to be there. I put on a tape of Johnny's new songs and they were really good. The tape player had a problem, however, and ate up the tape.

"Shit, Dee Dee", Johnny said to me, "that was the only copy of those songs! I'll never be able to remember them any more. Oh, well", and he laughed that crazy sick laugh of his, which sounded to me like someone's finger nails scratching down a chalkboard. "Fuck, man, the tape is ruined! I could have traded it to Billy my dealer for some blow!"

Finally, he got tired of complaining and we decided to walk back over to my apartment on 10th Street. When we got upstairs, he asked me if I had any spoons. Since I wasn't doing dope, I had a bunch of them. He took one and went in to the bathroom. Later, I saw the spoon. It was bent over and had been burned on the bottom of it to cook up some dope. A little piece of cotton, pink with blood, was still in the center of the spoon. I picked it up and threw it into the trash can by the toilet. What a bunch of loser friends I have, I thought to myself. It seemed to me that this Lower East Side low-life stuff had been following me around for ever.

After I left The Ramones, I didn't talk to the other guys. I didn't see anyone. As soon as the good times and the money were gone, it was just me again. No one wanted to know. The typical show business type of thing.

I know the Ramones management didn't know what to do with me. When I went to see Gary Kurfirst, he didn't have anything positive to say about me getting a new band together. Everyone at Sire Records was unapproachable. The only thing Gary could think of was that the Ramones might need some more songs, so he sent me to see Andrea Starr, who worked for the Ramones management at Overland. Andrea seemed to be on my side. She and I had always gotten along in the past. Andrea had also tried to help me with my *Dee Dee King* album, but it was in vain. My

Dee Dee King rap album was me trying to write in an imaginary way, not autobiographically—giving myself an assignment. I can write what I want to but I don't want to play the music business game. That's me. Dee Dee. But I could tell that Andrea didn't know what to do with me either. I guess everyone could tell that I was about to go through another bad period in my life, and they had their own troubles, so I was at the bottom of everyone's list.

Paris

Andrea was friends with Stiv Bators, who had recently left The Lords of the New Church. She suggested that I get out of New York for a while, and hook up with Stiv and try to start up a band in Paris. It was supposed to be with Chris from the Godfathers on guitar, Vom from Dr and The Medics on drums, and me on bass. I told Andrea and she said to discuss it with Stiv, which I did. I called Stiv in Paris and told him I'd come, but not if Thunders was there. I told him about what had happened the last time I was with Thunders, and Stiv agreed with me. So I flew over to Paris to stay with Stiv and his girlfriend Carol. It was OK, but a little creepy for some reason. It was always cold, and if I got a chill, Stiv would say, "Oh, that's just cause the devil is here with us."

Thunders was there too—there he was, sad, angry and mad, all at once. They also had a big black cat called Satan, which used the kitchen sink to go to the bathroom. Christ Almighty! And Thunders was doing everything possible to get me to do dope.

It's too bad. Thunders, Stiv and I could have had quite a band. We did try to go to one rehearsal together, though, but we just sat round and couldn't get it together. We each had an acoustic guitar, and were playing

1950's Dion and The Belmonts material. Nothing was really happening, though. Stiv was very broken down from his days in London and he told me that his liver was only 80% functioning.

Meanwhile, Carol was trying to run the show, pointing out everything we were doing wrong. "Put down that twelve-string, Stiv", she'd say to him. "No-one wants to hear any silly love songs from you." Carol does have good taste in music.

I could also tell that Stiv, John and I were not going to get anywhere as a "three guys from New York act." But I knew that I needed to do something, so I woke Stiv up and marched him upstairs, where I had a live mic and my stacks set up, along with a wah wah pedal and a distortion unit. I had my bass and I was ready.

"Stiv, I want you to shout SHIT! and FUCK! and PISS! into the mic as I am going at it, ok?

"Ok, Doug" Stiv replied. He had a happy/sad/I-am-confused face on, but lord knows what he was really thinking. I saw that same look on Brian James's face a year or two later at the Gold in Portobello in London. In fact Stiv was staring at a mouse that had been caught in one of their traps—there were so many mice and rats in the apartment that Carol had to put out traps because Satan couldn't catch all of them. The mouse was not quite dead, and was still twitching. Stiv caught its eye before it died, and said in a thick German accent:

"All good cretins go to heaven!"

I couldn't believe it, so I started playing my bass like a maniac possessed by some evil spirit. But I couldn't get Stiv to react. He couldn't stand up for too long any more, and he fainted. He tried to shout something once or twice, I'll give him that. But no cigar. Being in The Lords of the New Church with Brian James had fucked him up too much. I picked him up and carried him downstairs to his bed.

I didn't know that Carol was in the bed also, but she was. She lifted up the covers and peered at me. Her hair was dishevelled and her eyes were glowing like two yellow coals. Under the covers in the darkened room, she looked somehow like a snake. Carol was only half awake, but I had disturbed her and I knew she could be a hassle, so I decided to try to charm her.

"Oh, Carol, baby. Sweet darling, how are you? I was just finding some dope for you and Stiv, but I decided to bring Stiv to you first. Now I will run upstairs and fetch some dope. Then I will be right back. Carol, you would like some dope if I have some, wouldn't you? Don't worry, I have some. I'm going to fetch it now. Trust me."

"Oh, Dee Dee!", Carol shrieked with delight. "This sounds quite lovely!"

It was one of the first times I had ever seen her come so to life. When she smiled, I noticed something however—two fangs appeared to be coming out of her mouth! I had never noticed them before, and they reminded me that I had better get going while the going was good. I had been bullshitting Carol, though, and now I was in a trap because of my own stupidity. I had to make good and get the dope. Everybody was waiting. The whole household was disrupted and they were blaming me.

So, basically what happened is that I had to go back down there and meet them. Then we all played a game of Vietnamese Roulette, which is the same as Russian Roulette, except that the de-sensitization is done with opium instead of with lead. I loaded the poisoned hypodermic and fired it. It bit deep and filled me with intense hatred.

One of the last things that happened in Paris which really pissed me off was another bad scene between me and Johnny Thunders. A BAD one. I was convinced he had been stealing things from me ever since I had arrived, but I couldn't prove it. Then I caught him red-handed. My coat had gone missing and I found it in his suitcase. I don't care if he was Johnny Thunders or whoever. I was fed up with being so nice. I just lost it with all of them and made a big scene.

The next day I took a cab to the airport and bought a ticket back to New York. I had tried my hardest with Stiv while I was in Paris. I just couldn't get a break, though. I put the emphasis on trying to write songs with him, or get a band together with him and Thunders, but nothing worked. I couldn't penetrate the barrier that Stiv and Thunders had wrapped around themselves. It was like that in the Ramones. I couldn't penetrate the barrier around them either. Eventually the Ramones became a clique, and I felt excluded from it.

It was ridiculous, trying to please people who can't be pleased. I ended up friendless anyway. I knew that all my so-called friends back in New York would take Thunders' or Stiv's side over what had happened in Paris. In addition, no-one understood why I left the Ramones, and it wasn't a very popular decision. It was not going to be a very good time in life.

After I left Paris, Stiv politely tried to steal my song "Poison Heart". I had a tape of it in my suitcase. When I got back to New York, it wasn't there. Stiv went to England and recorded a demo of it. It would be too painful for me to hear the actual demo—after all, I am the only survivor of the three of us. Although at the time no one thought I would outlive Johnny or Stiv. As for Stiv, I always thought that behind his Joey Ramone shades and hairstyle, there was a punk rock singer, so I forgive him. RIP, Stiv.

The Liquid Concentration Camp

New York seemed very cold when I got back. If I wanted to break my isolation I was going to invite trouble. The Ramones had sort of been my family—now there was nothing. It was also a set up for disaster living on 10th Street again. Everybody in the neighborhood dealt dope—one of my old cocaine dealers even lived in the same building as me.

I never realised life could be so grim. Finally, when I hit the street I was lonely and tired of having conversations with myself. I started thinking that I could justify anything, so I started getting high again. All the dealers were more than happy to have a big spender around. They gave me attention and made me feel like I was very special. When I was stoned, I would sit on the stoop with them and spin fantastic tales about all my adventures to my new-found friends.

During September, when I went to the guitar shop on the Lower East Side, I noticed people selling dope in the area, so I went there to cop some. It was on 13th Street and Avenue C. There was an abandoned building on the corner where they sold heroin. The brand name for it was "bulldog". The dope had different brand names and if you were going to cop, you said you were going over to the Bulldog. It was more organised than in the early days of punk rock in New York City.

I started trying to re-live the old days. The old routine. Hitting the sidewalk around 12 o'clock to go cop. Then, on the way home, I would stop at the deli on 10th and First to get some coffee and some cigarettes. I'd try to avoid the street crazies and panhandlers, and as soon as I'd walk out the door of the deli, I would scurry down the sidewalk and up the stairs to my apartment. In my bathroom I'd shoot up like Thunders did when I had him over. The bathroom was a good place to get high and forget where you were. You could observe reality down below on the street if you wanted to. This is sort of traditional New York behaviour—staring out the window in a daze. I loved to do it.

It would always be real noisy and confusing down there. A madhouse of activity all day and all night—people hustling dope on the street. The customers want it, but it's cold. The freezing winter cold makes the chill in a junkie's bones even worse. No one's in the mood for any bullshit. In the city, it's animal eat animal. Man is a dangerous predator. You have to be on the ball. You risk going into debt to your supplier if something goes wrong. You risk going to jail.

Once, when I was looking out the window, I noticed four people who sold dope in the area. You could sense trouble coming. One of the guys down there was my old coke dealer, he was on the lookout for his girl so he didn't see the two enforcers who were about to come down on him. They were blending in with the crowd of street crazies and paranoid customers. It all happened so fast—one of the enforcers had a golf club and the other had a heavy walking stick. They were there to collect money owed to the supplier. They told the girl to hand it over, and started roughing up her man. Their two friends who were with them ran across the street to help, and then a car, which was parked nearby, pulled away from the kerb and stopped right in front of the action. The person on the passenger side of the car stuck a Marlin twenty-two automatic carbine out of the window. It had a banana clip in it, and he started firing it. At the sound of the shots going off, the whole block scattered. It was like a scene from a movie, but it wasn't. It was real.

The cop cars were there in a minute. I saw them grab the girl. She was in shock and just standing there. The police cuffed her and threw her in the van. The paramedics picked up her boyfriend who had been shot. They lost their dope, their money and their freedom.

I kept thinking, "Is this any way to live?" Is the system giving us any choice? It's so stupid. Society is burning itself out. American cities are hopeless and it doesn't look like it will ever level off. It makes me wonder how minority groups can survive, because it's even harder when you're hated all your life—no one will give you a break. You're judged guilty before they can prove you did the crime. You live in a war zone and have to fight constantly to survive.

When you're really down, you sense that someone is doing their best to keep the oppressed people oppressed. Drugs keep flowing into poor neighborhoods. It's the easiest thing for a government to do, because they see these people as a problem. They see them as a burden, not as human beings. Even though I was self-supporting, there were people claiming that I was a burden, so they came down on me. I was caught up in the big mess like everyone else—publicly and socially I was an outcast. Who the fuck would care if 10th Street in New York City burned down? We'd just stand there, watch it burn, and breathe in the smoke. Everybody could get one last high for free. What kind of a deal is that?

I only lasted a few months copping dope again in the East Village. I was 38 years old and caught a dope habit again and I couldn't handle it. For the first time in my life I had lost my freedom. I had to go on the methadone program for real. I became doomed to being a lifer in the liquid concentration camp.

Realistically I don't think anything else could have happened to me at that point. Too much had gone wrong. I had made too many changes without any support system. Instead, there were people really going for me, trying to take me down. Then I got the news that Stiv Bators had been in an accident and gotten killed in Paris. He was hit by a taxi. At about the same time, my best friend, Phil Smith, a pot dealer in New York, died of AIDS. Then, I found out my girlfriend was a whore. Finally, I got on the subway one day at Astor Place and took the Lexington Avenue local uptown to the celebrity methadone clinic on 69th Street and First Avenue.

I hated my life. I sort of wished I was dead. Being a methadone patient was like the end of the line. I had no choice. I had no Blue Cross insurance, so I couldn't get into a rehab. I tried to go to an AA meeting and a NA meeting, but they just put me in a worse mood. Especially the Artists' and Musicians' Meeting on St Mark's Place. There was just no way I was going to go cold turkey and stay off dope and live in the East Village. There were a million other reasons too, so the methadone progam was the best I could do to manage my life as a junkie at that point. Methadone didn't exactly put me in a good mood when I left the clinic and rode the subway back downtown. I always felt worse. That's why I started referring to the program as the liquid concentration camp.

In my weak state of mind, I was totally defenseless. On the surface, it might seem hard to believe that people would go out of their way to hurt me. I mean, why bother? Why? Because of my money. What could be more logical than for my enemies to run me around in circles until I was so dizzy that I didn't know what I was doing any more. The only way I could fix the pain was the only way I ever knew how—to run to the cooker. Drugs are the killer's dream. It's not fair, but that's how it is.

It was after I had been arrested twice for posession of pot that things took a turn for the worse. The first time I was defending my girlfriend on the subway. The second time I was walking by this club in New York called The Bottom Line. All of a sudden, the cops swarmed on me. They cuffed me and threw me into the police van. They picked up everyone who looked a little weird—it was a sweep. When the police van was nice and stuffed, they drove it to Washington Square Park and parked it by the fountain. The press had been notified ahead of time. That's why they made such a big deal out of it: so it would appear that the City was winning the war against drugs. That they had caught a hardened criminal. Me. Dee Dee.

They photographed me all the way to the precinct, and then threw me in jail. I was real fucking mad by then. I protested everything, which delighted them even more. The next day, my picture was on the front page of "The New York Post". Somehow that picture makes me laugh today. I looked like a madman, but then again, I was tattooed, ripped and unsmiling. I was real damn angry! I'm not a judge, and I do not think that weed should be illegal, anyway. But if I did have to be punished, what was the big deal, considering how harmless my crime was anyway? Lisa Robinson, the rock columnist of the "New York Post", who never had a good word for me anyway, wrote a piece about me supposedly passing out with a needle in my arm in the bathroom of this club.

Then the Ramones' management turned on me. They took advantage of my bad luck streak, and strung me along to get material for a new Ramones' album. I sold the publishing rights to "Poison Heart", "Main Man" and "Strength to Endure" for a few thousand dollars so I could hire a lawyer to get out of jail. I don't know why no one in New York, or none of the Ramones, couldn't have loaned me a few thousand dollars, instead of forcing me to go through all the paranoia, confusion and extra pain of a manoeuvre like that. And to top it off, these songs ended up on a new Ramones album called *Mondo Bizarro*.

It seemed that The Ramones couldn't live without me, but at the same time they treated me like an enemy. I considered it vain and stupid on their part, but it was probably the only way they could save face. To build up the Ramones, they had to keep running me down. In interviews they were obviously trying to play down my role as a writer—"Dee Dee co-wrote it." NO, I wrote it with all my heart and soul. "Poison Heart" was MY song about MY life.

At the same time, a hate campaign started against me. There were all sorts of rumors. That I was going crazy. That I was shooting pistols off on the street. That I stole a loaf of bread from the supermarket. That I was killing cats in my apartment. Everyone seemed to have their own idea about what I was doing. Nobody bothered to find out the truth from me—the only person I was having conversations with at this point was myself. I am pretty much anti-social anyway. Everyone else I knew was dead, or some kind of rock and roll casualty. I was lonely. The depression drove me straight back to drugs.

I felt like Public Enemy Number One—so I tried staying out of the East Village for a while. 10th Street was too hot for me, and I got a little apartment on 23rd and Lexington and tried to hide out. They had a methadone clinic in the neighborhood. The methadone patients were so stoned that they would stand on the street and wave in the wind. They never completely tipped over—somehow they would wake up for a moment and wave back the other way. They were real fucked up.

My friend Mark Brady was trying to lift me above this b-movie mentality. He was a good friend and a good influence on me at the time. I met him through Rachel Amado, who had the lead role in a movie which Mark was making, called "What About Me?" which also starred Johnny Thunders, Richard Hell, Nick Zed and Jerry Nolan. I wish Mark still had my phone number, and would give me a call.

Mark was trying to motivate me, so he gave me a small part in the movie. After we finished my scene, we called it a wrap and went over to Rachel's apartment to relax and smoke some weed. When we got there the phone rang. It was Stevie, the guitar player in Johnny Thunders' band.

"Rachel", he said, "John died. He's dead."

I was stunned. So was Rachel. Six months earlier Stiv Bators had died. My friend Phil Smith had just died. Life seemed so fragile. All the memories started flashing before me. They told me that Johnny had gotten mixed up with some bastards down in New Orleans, who had ripped him off for his methadone supply. They had given him LSD, and then murdered him. He had gotten a pretty large supply of methadone in England, so he could travel and stay away from those type of creeps—the drug dealers, Thunders imitators and losers like that. Life seemed pretty cheap at that moment. I got up and left. I didn't care if I died next.

No matter how many differences me and Johnny had, I was miserable when I found out that he was dead. Everybody seemed to be fighting a drug problem. There was all this finger-pointing going on at me, that I would be next. It really pissed me off, and I made a vow that I would not die because of drugs, just to spite my enemies.

But I was still out of control. I was trying my hardest, but the reality was that the methadone wasn't blocking my craving for street drugs. I was still hell-bent on self-destruction. Mark Brady was worried that I would go on a binge when Thunders died. He was right. I shot up quarter-grams of cocaine for a couple of days. Then I went over to the Continental Divide for a tribute concert for John. The warm-up band was a 70's Dolls type of band, with a guitarist who was a Thunders imitator. They were playing "Chinese Rocks" as I went in. I turned pale and left immediately. It was too much for me. Instead, I went down to the Bowery and got drunk. The next day I shot up some dope. I just didn't give a damn any more.

I hated my life. I was living in a flophouse on 23rd Street and taking the subway to the methadone clinic every day. In the morning I would get the "Post". In the afternoon I would go cop some pot. I needed to get myself into a rehab program, but I didn't have the money. It was the holiday season and Christmas was the worst. One of my neighbors didn't like the fact that when I stepped out of my room I would slam the door. I tried to reason with him. My lawyer had explained to me that if I was arrested a third time, I would have to go upstate to prison. I already had two arrests behind me—one of which was for felony assault. But I ended up kicking his ass in the hallway anyway. Then I bade him a Merry Christmas and went to the Scrap Bar to celebrate, as I had nothing else to do.

I ran into Lemmy from Motorhead. He took one look at me and he told me I looked terrible. I knew that. He didn't look so great himself, but I was always glad to see him. I was hoping that he had some drugs. He didn't, but he gave me a small loan, a beer and some free advice—"Get out of New York, Dee Dee. Go to Los Angeles."

So I went home and decided to go to England. Carol Bators gave me the information on how to switch programs, as she had done it many times. I guess that Carol knew every trick in the book. I got it together the best that I could. I scammed four bottles of methadone to take with me on the plane. Then I got in a cab and took myself to the airport. I bought a ticket, got in a plane and flew to London. I know that the only reason I am still alive is because I left New York.

Westbourne Park

The customs officials at Gatwick didn't want to let me into England even though all the drugs I had on me were given to me legally by a doctor. I have always felt the wrath of discrimination every time I cross a border. As for the treatment I have gotten at places like Gatwick Airport Customs, all I can say is that it was very demoralising.

Somehow, I made it through all that, found a taxi and got to Earl's Court, where my hotel was. I was worried about how I'd get to my program, because it was outside of London, in Hayes, Kent. I called Ira, my friend and business manager in New York, to ask him what to do. I was becoming overwhelmed, and when he suggested I take the train, I panicked. So I took another cab. English cab drivers are the worst, and they charge a lot—about the same as a fix. I wanted to get off drugs, so I just put up with it. I was very weak, and tried not to make small talk with the smiling freak who was driving me. He let me out in front of an old, haunted looking house, where the drug program was located. I rang the bell and waited by the door until the nurse let me in. I was taken up a creaky, winding staircase to see my doctor. He was a nice guy, but kinda nutty. He asked me to explain my demons, but I wouldn't say anything.

He was used to working with dishonest addicts and remained pretty cheerful. I got a three-week scrip for methadone. We said good bye and I promised to be good. The receptionist called me a cab. The fare was a third of the previous fare, which made me very happy. I took the cab to the Flora Hotel in Earl's Court, my new home for the time being.

The Flora was right around the corner from the Boots drugstore. I would go there every day, pick up a quart bottle of methadone and drink it, hidden in a Boots bag, in one of those red, London-style phone booths. That was breakfast. All I could think of was how low I had fallen. Doing drugs on the street again, and in a phone booth! Oh well, no one seemed to care what I was doing anyway.

The only person who talked to me, and seemed to care how I was doing, was Mr Jefferies. I met him at the prescription counter at Boots. He was an old junkie and had to walk to Boots every day on two crutches because he was a cripple. He was a real survivor, and a success, for his type. He had been on dope for thirty years and had gotten his first scrip at sixteen. He too had a room in one of the hotels around Earl's Court. He invited me to come over and hang out. He said that if I was ever stranded, I could crash on his floor. No one else had even talked to me, and here this guy was opening his door to me. I guess he needed a friend. I had learned a long time ago not to make friends, so I didn't really say that much to him. He had been around, and was the same type as me—a street rat. He asked me at once why I wasn't using the needle. That I could get anything at the program at this point. I told him that I wanted to quit.

"Why?" he said.

"You know why", I replied.

That was about it. Two social deviants struggling in the spider's web and pretty hopelessly trapped. I planned it that if I was still in England at Christmas I would go over to his room to celebrate.

Then, I met an Irish fellow in a pub who told me about a room available in Westbourne Park. He said it was a good deal, and took me to meet a German woman who wanted to rent it. When he showed up later to meet me by the tube station, he was fucked up on ecstasy—a drug I later decided that they should call "agony". It didn't matter, I was feeling better. I liked Westbourne Park. It was a nice working class area, and I liked the canal and the bridge. It didn't look like any place in New York. Perhaps the closest thing would have been Forest Hills in Queens. When we went over to the flat to meet the landlady, she said I could take the room. It was nothing special, and perhaps I would have been better off staying in Earl's Court. At least no one at the Flora was sleazy. But I had already made up my mind and I took the room. I didn't have to give her a deposit because she was so happy to have someone take the place off her hands. It was pretty crummy, but the best I could do. I was happy to have a roof over my head, and tried to make small talk with her. I guess she liked me, and we decided to go for a walk in the Portobello Road area, where all the flea market stalls are. On Saturdays this area would be buzzing and now I could walk to Kensington Market to look at clothes. I felt cool, like I was really living in London now.

I liked my new neighborhood a lot. There was a pub that we walked past called the Portobello Gold. It was described to me as "The Rockers' Graveyard", and I was told that it would be a good place for me to hang out and that you could cop dope in the area.

All the babes in London looked very flash, like they never do anywhere else. I was getting restless. One night, I cracked and took the tube to the Marquee to see the Phantom Chords. The Marquee Club was filled with vampire types, and with my colorless blood, plum hair and pale complexion, I fit right in. I started prowling around, and soon I spotted what would have been a perfect victim for me maybe ten years ago or so. She was all dolled up in a patent leather mini and spiked heels and she had that blond baby-doll hair. She looked like pure sex, but for once I turned down the chance for some excitement because I knew I couldn't take it. We were both too tired, anyway. She was worn out by her lifestyle. And life had just about gotten the best of me by then. We did hang out a bit, and the next day we went to see a movie, and went to Haagen Daaz for ice cream. As we were strolling around Piccadilly Circus, we passed a hotel, and the babe made some comment like, "Oh, there's the late-night bistro I go for a coffee when I'm in between jobs."

Well, the usual, right? I'd had enough of that in New York. I looked at that gorgeous creature, and though it was tough, I just said to her, "Oh, isn't that quite jolly", and scampered off towards the tube and just went home alone. I thought about calling her, but never did. I guess that's the price of recovery. You have to start trying to solve your problems instead of creating new ones. The officials at Gatwick had given me a chance to correct my mistakes. I felt as if they were rooting for me to win. I took the chance and did things right for a change.

I wasn't panicking about the thought of death, but something in me was demanding that it was my turn to live. I started defrosting the blood in me. I was gazing over the barbed wire and dreaming about getting out of the liquid concentration camp. It was pretty overwhelming, but I knew I had to change completely. I really felt alone in England, but that was what I needed.

Once, near the Canal Street Bridge, I noticed a group of skinheads. They looked great, dressed in their Doc Marten boots and lightweight army trenches. They were all amped up and ready to swarm in on a possible victim. I am seeing all this as I am walking along, and notice how gleeful they become when they spot a "vic". He looks like an unshaven drunk, and the skins don't like him. One of them walks up to him, and shouts "Good Morning!" into his ear. The next thing the skin did was to snatch the guy's cap from his head. I guess they were going to fuck with him, but he had a bald head. The skin gave him a wooden look and let him go. As I was watching this, I thought that maybe I should shave my head too. This is England, right? And this is a grim society which I live in. I am going to have to live by a few rules here, just as I did when I was in the Ramones. This society has no use for weakness. Only the strong survive, and the strong prey on the weak. This is an outlaw society. When you have "Made in England" tattooed on your skull, you live by rules that you learn, by having to fight your way through life, and it doesn't give you much choice.

I was trying hard to see something positive in the routine of daily life. I would buy The Sun and The Mirror at the tube station for the horoscopes, before walking down the Portobello Road to Notting Hill Gate. I would stroll around Kensington Market, and then I'd start back home. The Westbourne Park tube station is a center of low-life activity in the area, and there was always some pitiful sight that would sadden me a little more before I dragged myself home. A week or so before I left London, I was buying the papers there and I saw a beat-up blonde with a child, standing by the payphone at the station. She looked so out of it, so out of place. She was crying, and her big tears were raining down on her baby's face. I guess she'd had a fight with her old man. She had probably had to run for her life. She took her child with her, and now they had nowhere to go.

I walked past them and started on my way home again. As I was crossing over the Canal Street bridge, I noticed a man who I could sense was the guy she'd had the fight with. I would describe him as a "Disco Dan" type. He looked like he was trapped forever in re-runs of "Saturday Night Fever". He was a mess, and with his cheap, lopsided wig on his head, he was embarrassing to look at. He was throwing his life away, and it looked pathetic. He was dead drunk and looked like he had always been that way. I felt like putting him out of his misery and pushing him off the kerb and into the traffic. I knew that I was losing it.

It reminded me of something I had once read. An old drunken man, walking down 23rd Street pointed it out to me. It was written on the door frame of the Chelsea Hotel. I had never noticed it before. It read, "The man who says he hates you, hates the human race." That hit home. How could I go through life with so much hostility in me? I had to cut it out. No matter what had happened to me, I had to start surrendering in order to win. If everyone was my enemy, then I had to try and forget it for a while. I had to stop hating everybody. I had to stop hating myself.

I couldn't keep re-living my past and going through the whole routine over and over. I needed a chance to pull myself together. Seventeen years of touring with the Ramones hadn't been easy. When I was with them, we toured the world by rules that were decided for me—I had no part in mak-

Above: Johnny Ramone, Brixton Academy, London, 1996. *(Alan Giff, Ramones UK Fan Club)*

Above left: Joey Ramone at Top Of The Pops, June 1995. *(Veronica Kofman)*
Above right: Marky Ramone at home in Brooklyn, July 1995. *(Veronica Kofman)*

ing them. I was only allowed to learn them, live by them, and not question them. I had to learn how to just go blank and not think about it.

The Ramones became grim creatures on automatic. When Johnny Ramone would shout a command, we would listen. We would head to the theater for some fun. Whoever made the biggest fuss won. If you didn't win, there was always another game the next day. We were hardened pros. All we needed was a demon drum beat to rip to. When the smoke started fizzling and the speakers were about to blow, we would just stop dead on the beat.

The crackle on stage would get Johnny Ramone to freak out. He would get dangerous, yelling and glaring at everyone. He had nothing but pure hate in his eyes. He hated everyone, especially Joey and me. We loved it. It was fun to watch him go off. There are certain types who can really yell in an extremely hostile manner. I certainly can, my mother can, but John was fantastic at it. He could really make a sour face. In return I have pulled knives on him, yelled the f-word at him, and told him that I hated his guts.

Why we didn't stick together, I don't know. It's hard to get anywhere in life, and when we did, we just threw it all away. I just stood there on the stage, in the midst of all the insanity, and sulked. I knew that sooner or later a maniac lingering on the floor would slither up to me and say:

"Hey, man, wanna party?"

"What the fuck do you think, knucklehead? Dee Dee Ramone is my name. Drugs, booze and broads are my game. I am down with cocaine, beer, weed, wine and girls in mini-skirts. Also dope, valium and Quaaludes."

I knew that Johnny Ramone would be listening. I don't care, I thought. Is this a rock band or the fucking army?

In London I couldn't keep going to Boots every day any more. I got tired of the embarrassment of taking the garbage out when the only thing in it was empty methadone bottles, so I used to stack them up in the medicine cabinet. I also had a few full 90mg bottles sitting on the shelf in my kitchen cabinet. I had started taking it home and drinking it there.

It dawned on me that the only way forward was to slowly detox myself. I tried to be logical about what I was doing, but, looking back, it was probably pretty stupid to keep the methadone in my flat, but I felt insecure. Every methadone addict worries and worries... about earthquakes, or if there is going to be another world war and the hospitals and drugstores will close. So I kept it around. I wasn't tempted to drink a large dose and get loaded. Instead, I was getting very excited, sort of like I was out-racing the devil. The less methadone I had in my system, the more chance I knew I had, and I wanted to make it.

I started drinking three cups a day, which is what the bottle I brought home held. I kept a little chart on the wall, I was determined to get off the methadone, milligram by milligram. Soon I had a bunch of ugly, brown bottles, filled with green poison, sitting in my room.

Sooner or later I knew I was going to have to go home, so finally I called the accounting service that Ira had found for me to help me through my stay in London. I told them I needed to get home, so they sent a limo to pick me up, enough money to live on, and a Clipper Class ticket back to New York on Virgin Atlantic Airlines. I was a wreck, but I flew back to New York in style. There was even a limo waiting for me at the airport to take me back to the Chelsea Hotel, where I would be staying.

Before I left London I threw all that green liquid gook down the drain. I didn't want it to get into anyone else's hands. As far as I was concerned, my name was on the bottle, and in anyone else's hands it was illegal. I owed England something for letting me into the country, and this was my way of showing my gratitude.

Cold Turkey At The Chelsea

All's quiet on the Eastern front. Our east coast fort is quiet. There is an ice-cool breeze over the city. Sea gulls are gliding closer to the bay. There are new feelings in me. I don't feel I am a hopeless person, or that I should consider myself a loser.

New York in September has always excited me. It's when you can cruise the sidewalks faster. It's when the summer heat doesn't drag you down. I get Fall fever, but I am not sure what I am looking for.

It was August 28th, 1992, when I flew home from London back to New York. I was trying to hide it, but I was crying. I think I was crying because I realised I was almost 40 years old and had no home—nowhere to go.

After the plane landed at JFK, I hailed a cab to 23rd Street in Manhattan and checked myself into the Chelsea Hotel. I was lucky I had that. I knew I was going to have to suffer, but I had planned this. I knew what I was in for. To go cold turkey off the methadone. A fight for my life.

I refused all offers of dope from the friends that I used to know that still lived in the hotel. I locked myself up in my room and shut myself off from the whole world. I am stubborn, and was determined to make it through the withdrawal. I plugged up the cracks in the window in the bathroom and ran the hot water in the shower to steam the methadone out of me. Methadone doesn't lock in your blood, it locks in the marrow of your bones. It's difficult to kick. It's got to leak very slowly out of you. I did everything to help this process along. I shaved my head and clipped my nails to make it come out faster. I made myself eat and heated up soup on a hot plate. There was no one to take care of me. I kept thinking I really should be dead, but somehow I made it.

Finally, when I thought I could manage it, I decided to face New York again, and hopped into a cab to try and get some money from my publishers. If innocence is an illusion, then I don't believe it, because there is so much beauty in New York.

I hailed a cab at 57th and Broadway. The driver was a Puerto Rican girl, and she seemed cool. Latin girls always are. They seem to have a more realistic sense of urban survival than the type I used to end up with. She had her hair pulled back, a dark sweatshirt on and regular blue jeans. I got into the cab and politely asked her to take me to the Chelsea Hotel. We smiled at each other, and I felt relieved and glad that I didn't have a nut for a driver. I also felt something else, I'm not sure what. It was a new feeling. It was as if her pride was a turn-on—she was setting a standard for herself.

Les, one of the owners of Chelsea Guitars, the guitar store next door to the hotel, told me that Jerry Nolan was looking for me, and that Jerry was doing ok. Jerry, Les said, had written a story about his life for the "Village Voice". I wanted to see the story, but I wasn't ready to see Jerry. Everybody told me that he was off drugs and doing real well, but I was worried. Les told me that Jerry got five thousand dollars for the article in the "Village Voice". If he really has that much money now, I thought to myself, he won't be able to resist. It's too much temptation.

By the time Christmas came around I was crashing on the floor of Mark Brady's loft on 14th Street. We had no heat or hot water. I was very weak. Finally I went to the Astor Place Diner with Mark and another friend of ours to have Christmas dinner. Mine was a cheeseburger, and it looked mighty good. As we were eating, I saw Chrissy, my girlfriend at the time, stroll by the window with three tricks. She could almost have been the re-incarnation of Connie. They looked so incredibly alike. Oddly, this was the same neighborhood where Connie had died.

Even though I felt sorry for everyone, there was nothing I could do about it. I had tried that before. It just ended up bringing me to my knees. Then I would get high. I was lonely, but I was better off without her—Chrissy wasn't worth it. I had to escape drugs, prostitution and vio-lence. But it hurt. I loved Chrissy too.

When I was in England I remember reading something in The Mirror or The Sun which helped me. It was a story about a famous cricket player. His wife and he had broken up, then some reporters found out that his wife was on the game. What the reporters then did was to hire the girl for a photo session. It wasn't pretty. They splashed the story all over the front pages of the papers as well, and in detail. And then they went to interview him to get his reaction to all of this. I thought this would be enough for any man. They hounded him, and even interrupted him in the middle of a cricket match. And his reaction was,

"Excuse me, I have a game of cricket to play."

I thought this was a brilliant move and I copied it.

"Is that Chrissy?" I asked Mark and his friend.

"Yes, Dee Dee" they told me. "It's her."

They were upset. So was I.

"What do you think?" they asked me.

"Oh, I don't know" I said. "I have a cheeseburger to finish."

On Christmas Day, I sneaked into my old room in the building where I used to live before I left New York, on 23rd and Lexington. This was a real seedy apartment building, which used to be the George Washington hotel. By chance, one of my old girlfriends came by to see if I was there. She had a shopping bag with her, and I thought that she might have brought me a Christmas present, but she hadn't. She had just come over to add some more hell to my life. She started a fight, and then informed me that she was going to work over at the Executive Spa, a whorehouse on 23rd Street. Believe me, I didn't want a free sample. But I didn't get worked up and shoot dope over it. She was on the game—some things don't change. But I was changing, in my own way. I followed the "You make your own luck" rule.

What helped was that New York had become a big void for me. I didn't fit in. I couldn't relate. Walking around New York already felt like walking around a cemetery for me. Everyone I knew before had pretty much wasted their lives or were dead.

Then Jerry Nolan died. I cried over that. He was some kind of friend. I cared about him, and I looked up to him when I started playing. He had that cool, spiked blonde haircut. He was a star, at least in Manhattan, to Dolls and Heartbreakers fans like me. I couldn't go to the funeral. I just stood there in a daze after hearing the bad news from Mark Brady. Mark went to the funeral alone.

Mark didn't say much about the funeral when he got home. He was devastated. Jerry had also been a close friend to Mark, and Mark had tried to help him. Now it was too late. We both sank into a valley of pain that was becoming all too familiar. I could hardly breathe. I just ended up walking down one of the cold halls in our squat until I found a dark corner. Another person in my life had just become a memory. Pretty grim. What a business.

The Blues

For fourteen months after returning from England I had been trying to re-live my lower East Side past. I went to England to grow up—I had come very close to being a street junkie or worse. The creepy stuff that I saw along the way will always be in my memory. But some good came out of the sad things that happened. I don't think I would be doing anything if I hadn't seen what happened to Johnny Thunders. After he died, I knew I had to fight. The New York Dolls were a symbol of the old school of New York "rock" and I felt that with his passing, something else died too.

If all this sounds confusing, then how do you think I felt? I felt doomed. As an ex-Ramone, I was already too damaged by my past to expect any-thing else. Now I am just trying to get over my amazement that I made it through all that, and I am still alive. My life is getting better. I've been through a lot.

If you believe the old saying that you have to live the blues to play the blues, then I guess I am pretty damned experienced. Someone once told me that good things don't happen overnight. That things take time to de-velop. Well, I have also heard that saying, "Shit happens". I wanted to play the blues, because I felt the blues. It was a way of starting over from the beginning. It was an opportunity to retrace my life—a chance to change my old patterns. So I joined a rock group again. I began to learn self-control and to look at music as fun again. Just like when I was a fan of rock groups like the Rolling Stones.

I had it rough in the Ramones, but that was all over now. But at least it gave me a good background from which to judge my mistakes. I began to think that I could survive another round with rock'n'roll music. I knew it would take its toll. I was under no illusions. I didn't know if there was anyone in the music business who cared less whether I ever played another note of rock'n'roll again.

One of the things I realised was that the whole competitive thing about being in a band was boring. I wish all of us in the Ramones could have been cool, but we didn't know any better. We let the business push us around. It's a system that controls rebellion for profit, sort of like drug lords do. Originally, maybe it was different. Did Chuck Berry's "Roll Over Beethoven" stand for that?

It's hard getting a band started. I remember when I was in Gary Kurfirst's office discussing the musicians that might be available to start a band, he didn't have a good word to say about anyone. I don't want to mention any names, but he ran everyone down. Well, I could tell there was nothing happening. All he wanted was for me to write some Ramones songs for their next album.

Aggression is what drives a great rock'n'roll band. It can't be faked or it will be obvious crap. Upper class people can't understand that. The capitalist system can't create rock'n'roll bands and expect everybody to accept that as rebellion. That won't work. A system that protects one side, while the rest of us do time, is going to make me mad. So don't expect me to cooperate.

I was never even aware that there was a class system in America, until I moved to Ann Arbor, a town in Michigan, populated—dominated might be a better description—by rich, spoiled college students. One of the things that had attracted me there was the myth that high energy rock'n'roll came from Ann Arbor. I can still see how Liverpool gave us the Beatles, but I'll never figure out how Ann Arbor gave us Iggy and the Stooges.

Going to Tower Records every day kept my spirits up, but there was pretty much nothing to do there. I guess that's why I started to play the guitar again. I started out like everyone else, by learning old blues numbers, I thought I was going to be the next Johnny Winter or something. But I am what I am. I still just shake and smack the guitar around up there like Johnny Ramone does. I don't bother to play it. I think I use it to yell at everybody.

Since there was a blues jam in Ann Arbor at the Blind Pig every Sunday, I went there to see what was happening. Soon I started going there faithfully and jamming with the locals. On one occasion, I was just trying to mind my own business, struggling to get through an old Muddy Waters tune I had learned from an old blues cassette that I stole from a local Ann Arbor band's rehearsal room. When I ended the tune, Al Vicious, the bass player with the house band just stood there grinning, trying to be polite. The drummer and the harp player didn't know what to do, so I played it cool. I don't think anyone there thought that the blues should be played that dirty, but they were amazed and still wanted to see me do something.

Gary, who runs the jam at the Pig, came to my rescue. He strolled up to the bandstand, trying to make out like everything that was happening had actually been planned. He took the mike and announced that I would play "Wart Hog" for everyone. What the fuck?, I thought to myself. I counted out "One, two, three, four" and we started cranking it out. Everybody went home happy.

Back in the early eighties, my counselor at Odyssey House, Harold Holloway, tried very hard to reach me, but wasn't getting anywhere. Harold knew I was about at the end of my line. A lot of other therapists would have given me up as lost cause, but he tried his best. Finally, he tried to get me to write a love song to get me in touch with my feelings. He kept after me until I panicked. Finally, I knew I had to give him something.

"You want a song. I'll give you a song", I thought to myself.

The next day I gave him the lyrics to "Wart Hog":

I take some dope I feel so sick
It's a sick world, sick, sick, sick
Doomsday visions of junkies and fags
Artificial phonies, I hate it, hate it

Death, death, death is the price I pay
It's a sick world, what can I say
No such thing as an even break
It's stealing and cheating, take, take, take

Wart, wart hog
Wart, wart hog
Wart, wart hog
Wart, wart hog

I wanna puke I can't sit still
Just took some dope and I feel ill
It's a sick world, sick, sick, sick
It's a hopeless life, I hate it, hate it

It's a joke, it's a lie, it's a rip-off, man
It's an outlaw life, we're a renegade band
Doomsday visions of commies and queers
Artificial phonies, I hate, hate it

Wart, wart hog
Wart, wart hog
Wart, wart hog
Wart, wart hog

"What the fuck is this?", Harold asked me, looking at the piece of paper I had just given him.

"I don't really know", I replied.

I could tell he was pissed off. On my way out, I think I heard him say to himself, "Why are they all such knuckleheads?"

Well, anyway, on my way home that night at the blues jam, after I had just finished playing "Wart Hog", I felt myself getting the fever again. I could feel that old love of the spotlight stirring in me, so I started weighing the odds. If you do it, it hurts you. And if you don't do it, it hurts you. So there's not really a choice, I thought. Also, if I had a group, I'd have some people to hang out with again. I was lonely, bored and needed something to do. Finally I decided to do it. What the fuck, I thought to myself. I knew I could depend on Tom Templin, a local bruiser, to keep the band in line. Tom was from Detroit, so I thought I'd look for my new band members there. It was scary, but I knew I was going to do it. There was no turning back unless I wanted to be all alone, I still have to run with my own kind, and that's why I started The Chinese Dragons, and wouldn't you know it, I ended up singing "Wart Hog" every night again! What a goof.

For good measure I decided upon a "fuck everybody" attitude, and after a while I thought I'd play some Ramones songs and fit some blues songs into my show. "Wow, this is great", I thought. I was excited.

Before I went upstairs to my flat, I called an associate of mine at the Doug McAlpine agency from a pay phone near where I lived.

"Hi, Doug, it's Dee Dee. How ya doing?"

"How are things?" Doug said.

"Oh, everything's ok. Well, well, listen to this. I'm going to start a rock'n'roll band again and it's going to be from Detroit, like Iggy and the Stooges and the MC5."

"Wow" Doug said, "that's really something."

"Yeah, I know, it's going to be great."

Doug was an expert at blues and stuff like that. I met him at Solley's, a cocktail lounge in Deerborn, Michigan, where the blues bands play. He always tried to be polite, as he was trying to be now, but I could tell that was as far as I was going to get with him, even though he did get The Chinese Dragons their first gig at Solley's. I thought it was really cool for us to play a real blues club.

How it all happened though, was through Jeff Grant, a local guitar legend from Detroit. I met Jeff at a Jim McCarty and the Detroit Blues Band concert at the Paycheck Lounge in Hamtramik. Jeff took a liking to me, and started showing me around Ferndale, and I got to know the area around the Pay-Less drugstore, the Loving Touch Massage Parlor and the Coney Island place, where the Chinese Dragons and I would later go every night for dinner.

Jeff Grant had a little rehearsal room in Ferndale, not far from Gordy's Guitar Shop. He brought me up there one night, after we had been painting the town red. We had just come from Centerfold's, a local go-go bar, and we were both tipsy and feeling good. When we got upstairs, Richie, Allen and Scott were up there. Allen was as drunk as a skunk, and Richie and Scott seemed to be on another planet. This is great, I thought.

"You guys wanna play?"

"What do you wanna do?", they said.

"Oh, I don't know."

And that's how the Chinese Dragons started. It was about time Detroit stuck another rowdy rock'n'roll band on the universe, and I was glad to be on board.

So I got another chance to do what I've always done. I guess "Wart Hog" is my way of yelling at everyone who comes to my shows. People look at me with glee, but also like I am crazy, when I sing that song.

Buenos Aires

When I went to South America the last time around with my new band, I had a bunch of little creatures following me everywhere I went, as soon as I stepped out of the elevator and into the lobby of the fancy hotel I was staying at in downtown Buenos Aires. They all had Ramones t-shirts on, and were shouting questions at me, demanding autographs and asking me to pose for photos. I would feel myself start to flip, but I didn't lose it, and I didn't do any yelling, even at reception, or at the sneaky security guards patrolling the halls. I was imprisoned in the hotel room again, but this time I wasn't chained down by a cocaine hangover. I'd come a long way. I even went down to the pool and sat there under one of those umbrellas in the sun, and tried to relax.

I could have had all the cocaine I wanted, but I turned it down. I am just happy I don't have to suffer like that any more. Then I started to feel very gleeful that my idea of a party is a little more jaded than when I first came to South America. Actually, the thought that I was going to make some money for a change was a big kick to me. I had a laugh. "Boy, am I nuts" I thought to myself. Well, I guess that's what makes me so lovable.

Going back to Buenos Aires with my new band, I couldn't believe how loved the Ramones were. Their presence is a very intense influence on the kids down there. I guess because the Ramones and their fans come from the same sort of situations. Certainly not the same one some spoiled student is coming from in Ann Arbor. Then I could tell that if the Ramones were put into the position of representing something of some learning value, it is that there is hope and that it is possible to rise above oppression. That kind of stuff really makes me know that it's worth it to keep playing in a band.

In Argentina, I sneaked out of the hotel and got caught by a load of kids who surrounded me and started asking me questions. We sat down on the stoop, just like I used to with my "brudders" in Forest Hills a long time ago. We got talking about the Ramones and stuff, and then the conversation turned to guitars.

"Dee Dee" one of them said. "You play guitar in the old style."

Then one of them asked me what it was like when I first started playing.

"Well, you know, we used to get one of those old guitars and clamp a pick-up on it, then plug it in our mom's stereo when no one was home."

They couldn't believe it.

"That's what we do too, Dee Dee."

Christ, is this 1964 or 1992?, I thought.

We went to the theater to do a show for TV. It was a riot. During a break in taping, I wandered off to the side of the stage and hid behind the curtain and spied on the other band that was on the bill. From what I could tell, they seemed very New York-influenced. They had a Johnny Thunders type on guitar, counted "one, two, three, four" like the Ramones, and sounded like the Pistols. When I saw the singer's broken teeth, I knew where they were coming from.

Holland

Somehow, the last thing I needed was to get involved with any more in-sensitive music business types, like the promoter based in Nihagen, who first invited me to the Netherlands where I formed a somewhat messy musical project called ICLC. I was on my own, and for nine months I lived in a cheap hotel room in the Rembrandt, next to the train station in Venlo, a small border town in Holland. I liked Venlo, but I could tell it didn't like me. It was made very obvious to me. So, I moved again, this time to Amsterdam.

My first apartment in Amsterdam was on Rosen Straat. Amsterdam is a beautiful, tree-lined village-like city. It has a very free spirit, and it's not a place to go and try to get serious. But that's what I did, and it didn't work. The apartment on Rosen Straat had a machine shop underneath me. The drilling was driving me mad. I piled carpet after carpet on the floor to try to deaden the noise. I found used carpets in the garbage that dogs had shit on too many times, and took them to the dry cleaner. After a good washing, they were completely re-usable. Finally, in an all-out effort to block out the noise from the street as well as the sounds of yelling children from the playground downstairs that filled my apartment all day long and steadily shattered my nerves, I went to the Block Hamm department store in the Haag, and I bought some rolls of transparent blue plastic tape, with which I wrapped up the whole of the inside of the apartment.

Finally the tension got to be too much for me, and I had to move again. I got a new apartment on Harten Straat. That didn't turn out to be much better. It wasn't exactly the street where I was living that was bad. It was the whole city. I realised then that maybe the whole European attitude towards Americans is pretty bad.

In Holland, in two years, I didn't make one single friend. It got so bad in Amsterdam that in the summer, if I wanted to get out of the apartment for a while for some air, the best place to go was to sit on the edge of the sidewalk next to the canal and try to hide myself from the passing American-hating citizens of Amsterdam.

To make things worse, The Ramones were still together. They even did a live show on MTV whilst I was living in Amsterdam. It seemed like any little thing they did ended up causing me grief. They looked horrible on MTV—so old, tired and angry. Even though, I hadn't had anything to do with them, it was hard to get that Ramones stamp off your head, for some reason. I guess it's the curse of fame. After the show on MTV people started making smart-aleck remarks to me around town. Why does Joey seem so fucked up? What is he on? Why didn't he sing? Why did CJ sing? and so on. The general opinion in Amsterdam was, "Why do they bother any more?"

Then they went and booked a date in Rotterdam and everybody was asking me if I could put them on the guest list. Can you imagine that? Two beautiful Dutch girls even tried to pick me up and trick me into having sex with them. I couldn't believe it. They wanted to be with me so they could get to meet Joey Ramone! I was getting sick of so many girls doing that to me. Even my new girlfriend Barbara was a big Ramones fan. She even named all her toy dolls and animals Dee Dee when she was in Buenos Aires. She really wanted to go to Rotterdam to see them play.

I had met Barbara on my previous tour of Argentina—she was from Buenos Aires. Eventually she flew out to Holland and joined me in Amsterdam, after much wrangling with her parents, and with the authorities about residence permits. After all, she was very young. In the end she had just about persuaded me to go to the show in Rotterdam, when we received a Ramones fanzine in the mail. In it was an interview with Johnny Ramone and they asked him if the Ramones ever did a last show together, would they have me come up on stage and play with them.

"No", he replied, "CJ is our bass player now."

Well that was true and, I wasn't instigating anything about playing a last show with the Ramones, but the show in Rotterdam was rumored to be their last. So, everybody in town started hassling me to go play with them. It was insane. In the end I let it be known that I would be in New York the day they were playing in Rotterdam. I also told them that I would, however, be in Rotterdam to hang out afterwards. It was all very touchy because they wanted more songs from me again.

Instead I took Barbara to the Milky Way, the Milkweg, a club I had played with The Ramones on a number of occasions. By now I was getting used to the dirty looks and strange treatment that I received when I went out. I guess it doesn't help having a beautiful young girlfriend when you're 43 years old, but that's my style. What can you do, right? Amsterdam felt like my last stand. I had been on the run for five years since I quit the Ramones, and I was tired of running.

As soon as Barbara and I got comfortable by the bar, a horrible, creepy young little girl slithered up to me and said:

"Are you like Bill Wyman, the loser of the Rolling Stones?"

"I really don't throw sweets to babies", I replied. I was really just trying to get away from her, but she was clever. She was right in my face, trying to stare me down, waiting for my reaction so she could get a good giggle from it all.

Well, I looked at her hardened, mean, little-girl face, and I attacked. I got in the first giggle, with a finely executed, bitter-sweet smirk that I have often practised. Then I brought my hand up to my mouth, cupped it, and let go with a cough into her face, and then added, "You must be the loser of the Milkweg."

Soundchecking for the last-ever Ramones show.
Hollywood Palace, Los Angeles, August 6th 1996 *(Veronica Kofman)*

Dee Dee Ramone, Marky Ramone, CJ Ramone - "The Remains". *(Barbara Zampini)*

Then I spun around on my heels and smart-marched Barbara in the opposite direction, so as to regain my composure.

"I've had enough. Come on, baby. Let's go home", I said.

I promised I would take her to see the Ramones at CBGB's in New York. I happened to know they were playing there again to make some money to pay Marc and CJ and the road crew, and a few other band bills.

On the way out of the Milkweg, I heard an angry voice curse me in Dutch. As I turned around I saw that it was that same creepy bitch who had just ranked on me about Bill Wyman. Well, if they can't be nice, then why should I be? That's the way it goes. Did they expect to push me around and that I was going to end up all friendly? No way. Maybe Bob Hope would, but not Dee Dee Ramone. No way! I can't wish anyone luck if they can't wish me any.

"The next time the Ramones play Rotterdam, I'll put you on the train and send you backstage to meet Joey Ramone, ok?", I told the little creep as we exited the premises. Of course, I wasn't telling the truth, but this was getting to be a goof for me.

I told her that the pinhead who brings out the Gabba Gabba Hey sign is still worth seeing! That pinhead will never leave them! He's got the John Merrick lifestyle—fame and pinhead bitches to boot.

Finally I said, "You know what though, you creep? You would be blessed if you could get up close and kiss his pointy head! Now get lost!"

Barbara and I walked along the Keizersgreacht to our little apartment on Hartenstrat, the stars were all out, and the sky was beautiful. I felt OK. "What a *lovely* evening", I said.

Barbara asked me, "What did you do after you played your last show with The Ramones?"

"Well", I said to her in an almost fatherly way, "you know what I did? After I put my bass down for the last time, I walked over to the pinhead and rubbed its head for good luck. And that was it. I hope my dear brothers do the same thing. They're going to be needing all the luck they can get."

As I walked the rest of the way home I suddenly said, "You know what? I do feel lucky. How could everything turn out so well for someone like me? It's amazing!"

Mechelen

A year has gone by since that walk back from the Milky Way. Finally, I
had to get me and Barbara out of Amsterdam. Another American couple
we met told us that the only way they could survive living there was to try
to stay invisible. I could relate to that. I wasn't happy about it. I felt like
I'd been tarred and feathered and run out of town.

As a result I moved to Mechelen near Antwerp in Belgium with Barbara and two dogs we had acquired along the way, Kessie and Babita.
Kessie was a mean street dog and very grouchy. Kessie also hated Amsterdam, and was always acting up on the street. Back in Argentina Barbara had a pit bull named Doogie, so after a while, I decided that I'd better
get another dog. So we got Babita, who was some kind of small Doberman and Rottweiler mixture.

I could have been very happy in Mechelen. True, it was boring, but we
had a nice place to live and it was quiet. It's sort of like the Ann Arbor,
Detroit, area of the USA. It's very strange being a New Yorker in
Mechelen. It's sort of medieval there. Cathedrals, cobblestone streets,
hand-painted signs, coats of arms, and on Sundays there's absolutely no
signs of life.

Also, the Belgian people are a lot friendlier than the Dutch. However, the Belgian police are a bunch of sick bastards—they were on my case almost as soon as I got there. They acted a bit like how I always imagined the really rough-necked southern State Troopers were like in Alabama during the height of racial tensions in the deep south during the 60's.

As soon as I moved to Mechelen, I got a lawyer in Antwerp to get me a residence permit. He suggested that for ten thousand dollars, I could start a publishing company that would qualify me for a permit in Belgium. It sounded good to me. I was happy, and said, "OK, let's do it." Michael from Herzog and Strauss immediately sent him all the papers, but my lawyer presumably never got started on my case. His grouchy assistant told me that she had filed Barbara and me on a police report, and that we would be OK until the papers came in. I asked her if we should leave Belgium first, to make things legal. "No", she snobbishly replied. "Stay here in Belgium where you are safe."

Safe, my ass, as I later found out. The only people who really ever seem to know the law are the police.

I had that worried feeling. I could sense trouble was coming my way, and, as usual, I was right. Barbara and I were almost deported from Belgium. One morning the cops picked us up in Mechelen when we were coming out of the newsagent with the morning papers. For no reason at all, they just forced us into their patrol car and took us to the station. They would not let me call a lawyer. They seemed so full of unnecessary hatred towards me and Barbara. They threatened us. They gave us an alternative—you can go to the USSR or Czechoslovakia, but you are on the computer with a violation of the laws of the European Community. We had to go. We lost everything we owned. I did not have any drugs on me—I didn't do them at all any more. I didn't have a weapon on me. I hadn't even committed a traffic offense.

My lawyer in Amsterdam told me that I was picked up for nothing, that the cops in Mechelen are like that. He told me that no American would be safe living there. I quite agree with him now. I have also learned my lesson and will never repeat that same mistake again. I will never go back to Belgium.

Then, one day my mother called. It was weird. I hadn't spoken to her in at least four years. My ex-management in New York gave her my number. She sounded alright, and I was glad she called. I told her that I wished that I could go back to Germany to live, but it was hard because I needed a residence permit and couldn't get one. She couldn't help. She lost her German citizenship and couldn't live there for more than six months a year any more. She gave me my grandmother's number in Berlin, and I called her. She really sounded off the wall. I could really see now why my mother was like she was when I was younger. Going through World War II, the bomb raids, the Russian invasion, her family, my father for a husband, it can't have been easy for her. Oh, and I hate to admit it—for her to have *me* for a son. But whatever sympathies I had for her, the wall around my emotions will always be there. I ended up telling her that my family is the Ramones. That I am Dee Dee Ramone, not Douglas Colvin. I never was much of a family man. Still, I felt alright about talking to her and after we hung up I bet we both felt the same way. All she or I can depend on is ourselves.

Just before leaving Belgium, I had to start a band to tour Spain. If I'd have pulled out, I would have gotten sued, so I had to do the tour. It was pretty stressful. Everyone in the music business seemed to be getting more and more dishonest and more and more full of crap than ever. It was one of those tours that was all for nothing. After the tour, Barbara and I boarded a plane in Madrid and flew home to Argentina. Finally, I had to get me and Barbara out of there.

Argentinian Farewell

I am sitting in a room now. It isn't mine. I am in Argentina again. A sleepy neighborhood in Buenos Aires called Banfield, at my girlfriend's grandmother's house. I am hiding again because I am feeling miserable and I know I will only make anyone else miserable who sees me, so I am giving all concerned a break. I do something stupid and let a dog wander in here, thinking he might cheer me up. I met him outside by the gate, and I have already gave him the name Ramon. He's a fat old street dog that has obviously been in a fight with another dog and has a slightly wounded leg. I have a slightly wounded head. I have had a fight with a Ramones' fan.

Barbara's grandmother and her two sisters met us at the airport. They put us up in Barbara's sister's room—she ended up sleeping in the living room. It got a bit edgy right away. I think I even might have driven everybody out of their minds, so here I am, sitting alone again in a room, writing. When I try to walk out into the outside, the world gets too intense for me. It makes me cringe. I feel vulnerable, out of place, and unwelcome everywhere I go. I feel shitty, like a criminal would feel, except I am not a criminal.

At this point, Ramon, the dog that I let in here, gets up and exits the room. He manoeuvred his way in here. Ramon had to get his way. So I let him in. I wish he would appreciate it. Instead, I got caught up in the inside, thinking about outside. I know Ramon is just an old abused dog, and how would he know what's happening, but it still bothers me. You fat bastard, I mutter under my breath as he duckwalks out the door.

What I needed most now was a visa for Barbara, so we could go to America, where I now felt that we would both be better off. But that would take another year of trying over and over. It was difficult. She was under-aged and had an Argentinian passport, and her parents wouldn't help us without major struggles. The red tape you go through in Argentina is rough.

In Argentina, it's like a time warp. It reminds me of when America was a nice country to live in. Even though everything is harder in Argentina, the people are nicer there than most places. The air is so smoggy that it cuts up your lungs. Bus drivers there are out to kill. They try to push people on mopeds off the highway on purpose with their big smelly buses. It's a madhouse. Everybody is blowing clouds of black smoke out of their exhaust pipes into each other's open car windows. Everybody's car window is open because no one has air-conditioning. The cars here are all old and fucked up, but have a lot of soul. It's very funky.

The hassles become mucho to get money to live on in Argentina. My accountant, Ira, used to send me money via the Western Union on Cordoba and Suipacha. The cab ride to get there was always a nightmare. First of all, it was hot. Very, very hot. Then, the cab driver would start chattering in Spanish non-stop about the Ramones. I can't understand a word. I mutter "si" to him once in a while. I am trying to keep my head, but since my driver's head is always turning round to talk to me and his eyes are never on the road ahead, I keep a fixed glare out the front windshield, sort of trying to will the taxi through the maze of traffic, determined that we won't fuck up and have an accident, because I have to get the money. The traffic is bumper to bumper. Stop and go. Nut job angry Latin drivers. It's like in a movie.

There are also police road blocks along the highway. When I get to Western Union, I run in and come right out with six 100 peso notes. I jump back in the cab and head back to Banfield in the outskirts of Buenos Aires, my current address. I should be happy, but I never get any peace. As we're driving along the news came on the radio that The Ramones are due to play their last show in Buenos Aires on March 16th. Iggy is also on the bill. Something always ruins everything. Right now it's the Rock and Pop station. They are advertising the Iggy and the Ramones show non-stop.

Then there's an announcement that Attack 77 have been added to the show. This really sucks. I'm not in the mood to see Attack 77 or Iggy's stupid face, or John, Joey and Marky's stupid faces either. And, as soon as I am out of the taxi, I storm back inside my place and turn off Rock and Pop, which Barbara has on full blast on a Panasonic boom box. What a shitty day. It's also a blow that the Ramones might be sticking around for a re-match. What a drag it all was.

It was becoming obvious that I was under some obligation to everyone to try to play at the final show with the Ramones. Everybody in the neighborhood started pestering me for tickets. I had to take out my guitar and play a few Ramones songs for everybody on the sidewalk in front of my home to keep the peace. It was horrible for me. I was really becoming demoralised. By the time the Ramones landed in Buenos Aires International for their last-ever show, I was wishing I were dead. I ended up promising to try and get people free Ramones tickets. I called Rock and Pop, the Ramones' promoter in Buenos Aires, nine times. I spoke with a few different people there. They couldn't promise me anything, except that they would call me back. They never did, so I guessed I wasn't going to go to the concert. That I had called Rock and Pop nine times and they were so rude made me feel like the whole world was against me. What else could I think?

Anyway, I guessed it might be too demoralising to see Dee Dee Ramone fans spitting at CJ instead of me, and to see the audience giving

Playing bass at Joey Ramone's birthday party at The Continental, New York, May 19th, 1997.

Johnny Ramone a hard time by trying to get him to make a mistake so he would get even angrier.

There was a lot of anger surrounding the show before it even happened. There was a riot in downtown Buenos Aires, when a ticket giveaway was inexplicably ignored by the promoter of the concert. None of the winners got their free tickets, after they had been standing in line all night to wait for them, so they got angry. It really made me not want to go after that.

I saw the whole thing. I had just been to Western Union to get some money and was on my way to the Dunkin' Donuts store to buy six tickets for Barbara's sisters Sofia and Rocio and their friends. The fact of having to buy the six Ramones tickets made me feel funny—I didn't know that they would be giving tickets away next door at the Coca Cola building. By the time the police arrived to clear everybody out, every store window was broken. Later on, the riot was reported on MTV.

Then Monte finally called me. After that I got to speak on the phone with Johnny Ramone.

"I don't know how we got stuck doing the Metallica tour, Dee Dee", he was going. "I am half crazy. Everybody's blown out. Arturo got busted for something right before we left for Brazil. It's been a nightmare. I wish you would come to the show. We'd like to see you."

"OK", I said. I felt terrible after I got off the phone with him. Despite all my troubles, I felt sorry for John and the rest of the Ramones.

I arrived at their hotel at five o'clock, the time that Monte had arranged to meet me. The band and I were going to do "53rd & 3rd" together at the concert. We were going to go over the song at soundcheck and then go for dinner and hang out.

This all sounded fine. What they didn't know is that for the last couple of days I had been trying to get inside the American Embassy to get a visa for Barbara, so I could take her to New York. I started my day at five in the morning, as I had to be waiting in line outside the Embassy by six. I might be crazy. I don't know. Whatever I am, I am not a good loser. I will fight and fight for what I want. People always say about me "Oh, Dee Dee, he always gets his way."

My mother and I have some kind of evil German clandestine arrangement—believe me, it wasn't my father who taught me how to fight. Finally, I was at such a loss that I called her up and said, "Mom, what should I do?"

"Go in there and fight and yell, that's what I did at the Embassy in Florida, Dee Dee. Then they paid attention to me, and I got my way."

So that's what I did. The day of the Ramones show, I went to the Embassy first thing in the morning. It was already crowded. I walked up and down the sidewalk casing the line a few times, but my nerve was up. I marched myself right up to the cop guarding some sort of mysterious bunker-like entrance through the gate.

"I want to go in there and get a visa", I demanded.

When I was at the second electronic search gate, I tried to slip them 300 pesos, but they wouldn't accept.

"We don't do that any more, señor", they said.

What got me the visa eventually was yelling just like my mother had told me to do. I should have had a party to celebrate, but I had the taxi let me off in front of the Hyatt Hotel to meet the Ramones. Because of the crowds, the driver would not stop. I had to open the door and jump out. I paid him later when I got back to Banfield. Barbara, who was not supposed to come, was right behind me. It was too much.

The hotel was fenced off by a security gate. There were police everywhere. Fans all over the place. The promoters were outside the hotel. They saw me and gave me a dirty look. Still, I tried to attract their attention.

"It's Dee Dee", I shouted. "It's me."

All the Ramones fans started agreeing, and shouting "It's Dee Dee. It's Dee Dee. Let him in." But they were pulling me back away from the gate and demanding autographs and photos.

The police were glaring at me with pure hatred. Everybody started to bum's rush me. It was like a tidal wave coming at me. By chance, I spotted Marky. I tried to get his attention. "Marky, help me!" I shouted.

He pretended not to see me. He was hiding behind the dark Elvis-type sun glasses he was wearing. He had spun a web of hate around himself.

With his black wig, black motorcycle jacket on, and his pale white skin, he looked so much like the original Marky Ramone that it was unreal.

He was standing outside the hotel, protected from the fans by the security gate. When the Ramones fans saw him, they flipped. I was out there alone. It was obvious that Monte had arranged for them to sign autographs at the same time as he had told me to be at the hotel. I had to fight for my life. It was horrible. Somehow I squashed Barbara and myself between the security guards, the police and the fans. I was dodging sharp pencils and pens being thrust towards my eyes by autograph seekers, and then someone kicked me in the shins. When I finally made it into the hotel lobby, I was pissed off.

Marky was the first person I saw.

"I hate you", I shouted. "You saw me, and didn't let me in."

"It's not true. I didn't see you, Dee Dee bunny chicken. Kiss me. We love you."

This sucks, I thought to myself.

Monte was there. He looked real blown out. It was sad to see him like that. Marc was trying to smile. It was that Hollywood showbiz practised look of concern smile that makes me feel even crazier when I look at Marc's crazy face. I was losing my grip. He's as insane as Monte, I thought to myself.

I saw Johnny Ramone and I was quite taken aback. This is serious, I thought. He looked very, very bad. Really terrible. Very blown out. I felt horrible about what I was seeing. This is not right. I was concerned about Johnny Ramone in the same way as I was about Brian James a few years ago when he did the final tour with the Damned. But soon I pulled myself together, and started to feel more cheerful. This is great, I thought. Barbara and I ended up having dinner with them in the lounge area of the hotel. A few privileged Ramones fans got to pester me while I tried to eat and talk to a worn-out Joey.

"Dee Dee", Marc asked me, "what did you order?"

"Oh, you know, Marc", I replied, "a steak sandwich and French onion soup. The most expensive things on the menu, you know, Marc, trying to get the most out of it as I can."

"I know what you mean, bro", he lovingly confided in me. I could tell that under his calm demeanor, Marc was secretly planning a comeback some day.

It made me feel good. How could I dislike this guy, I thought. After dinner, I went to the soundcheck in the van with the promoter and the rest of the band, except for Johnny Ramone, who was too miserable to be with Joey and Marc, so he went alone in a car with Eddie Vedder and his friends.

When they got to the stadium where they would be playing for 90,000 people, everything was ready for them. They took their positions and started checking. The group might have seemed impressive to other people, but not to me. They were good, but they had lost their cool. Johnny Ramone seemed more like a tennis player than a guitar player, you know.

In the end, I didn't stay for the show. I hadn't exactly received the royal treatment from the Ramones, their fans or Rock and Pop. I tried to be good about a real bad situation—to remain loyal after all the aggravation I had been through. But it didn't work. Fuck them, I thought to myself. On the way back to the hotel, I opened the door of the van and as soon as we stopped for a red light, I jumped out. I hailed a cab and before anyone knew what had happened, I was on my way back to Banfield, to Barbara's grandmother's house. Her sisters, Sofia and Rocio, were fighting so bitterly over who would go with who with the four tickets that I had given them, that I gave the other two tickets that Rock and Pop had given me to them to keep the peace. So I didn't go to the show. Instead I listened to it in my kitchen on the radio, tapping nervously with my nails on a red linoleum-topped table.

I felt there was no excuse for the way I had been treated. It was pretty inconsiderate to ask me to go to the show to play a song with them, set a time to meet me, and then take no responsibility for what happened outside the hotel when I went to meet them.

So many of these weak handshake type of incidents had left me very bitter towards the fans and The Ramones. There was so much harassment in the band about a possible Ramones documentary that was supposed to be filmed around their last performance, that I left them to it—left them my phone number and said I would make myself available. Somehow I knew it would never happen.

A Ramones story can't have a happy ending. I'm just glad it's over with, though some of it's been fun. I really don't think The Ramones should play together again. I say that not out of meanness, it's actually out of concern for them, and myself. I wish everyone in the band good luck. Because of our relationships with each other, we're all damaged. We hurt each other. My book tells the story—it's some story and I'm glad I told it.

My wife Barbara and me, New York, May 1997. (Bob Gruen)

Epilogue

On August 6th 1996, Dee Dee Ramone performed one last time with The Ramones. It was fitting that he should be there for the last performance of the band he co-founded in 1974. It may not have been a perfect ending, but the circle was completed.

At present Dee Dee Ramone continues to write, perform and record music. Joey, Marky, and CJ Ramone are pursuing solo careers. Johnny Ramone has retired.

I have been thinking how fitting it would be to end with a quote from a Ramones song: there are many that would have been appropriate. But I shall leave you, with these words from another band that shook the world—"And in the end, the love you take is equal to the love you make".

Veronica Kofman.

Album and single from
Dee Dee Ramone
on Blackout Records

Single: I Am Seeing UFOs (released on October 13th)

Album: Ain't It Fun (released on Oct 27th)

Dee Dee Ramone is back with a punch... and a bunch of 13 new songs,
friends old and new, and the same punk attitude that has made him such
an anti-hero and NYC street legend.

THE ONE AND ONLY: Peter Perrett - Homme Fatale by Nina Antonia
ISBN: 0946 719 16 0.
224 pages (illustrated). £11.95

An extraordinary journey through crime, punishment and the decadent times of The Only Ones. Includes interviews with Perrett and all ex-band members.

"Antonia gets everyone's co-operation and never loses her perspective on Perrett". **Mojo.**

"Antonia is the ideal chronicler of Perrett's rise and fall. From his time as drug dealer, to the smack sojourn in The Only Ones, Perrett's tale is one of self-abuse and staggering selfishness". **Select**

Plunderphonics, 'Pataphysics and Pop Mechanics by Andrew Jones
ISBN: 0946 719 15 2.
256 pages (illustrated). £12.95

Chris Cutler, Fred Frith, Henry Threadgill, Ferdinand Richard, Amy Denio, Lindsay Cooper, John Oswald, John Zorn, The Residents and many more....

"The talent assembled between Jones's covers would be interesting under any rubric. Thought provoking and stimulating". **Mojo**

"Jones's book is perhaps the first study of the growth of these techniques within the avant-garde. Packed with fascinating interviews and written with wit and insight". **Q magazine**

Dark Entries - Bauhaus and Beyond by Ian Shirley
ISBN: 0946 719 13 6.
200 pages (illustrated). £11.95

The full gothic rise and fall of Bauhaus, including offshoot projects, Love and Rockets, Tones on Tail, Daniel Ash, David J and Peter Murphy. Ian Shirley unravels the uncompromising story of four individuals who have consistently confounded their detractors by turning up the unexpected.

"A trench-to-toilet missive of who did what, where and when. It works brilliantly". **Alternative Press.**

"Solidly researched account of goth-tinged glam". **Top magazine.**

Wrong Movements - A Robert Wyatt History by Mike King
ISBN: 0946 719 10 1.
160 pages (illustrated). £14.95

A sumptuous and detailed journey through Robert Wyatt's 30 year career with Soft Machine, Matching Mole and as a highly respected solo artist. Packed with previously unpublished archive material and rare photos. Commentary from Wyatt himself, Hugh Hopper, Mike Ratledge, Daevid Allen, Kevin Ayers & more.

"King's careful chronology and Wyatt's supreme modesty produce a marvellously unhysterical, oddly haunting book". **Q magazine**

"Low key, likeable and lefty. Like the man himself". **iD magazine**

No More Mr. Nice Guy - The Inside Story of the Alice Cooper Group
by original guitarist Michael Bruce and Billy James
ISBN: 0946 719 17 9.   160 pages (illustrated). £9.95

Michael Bruce opens the lid on his years with the platinum selling group, revealing the truth behind the publicity stunts, the dead babies, the drinking, the executions and, of course, the rock 'n' roll.

"I'm Eighteen changed Alice Cooper from the group that destroyed chickens to the group that destroyed stadiums". **Village Voice.**

"It might even be argued that the band defined what it meant to be a role ridden seventies teenager". **Rolling Stone**

Wire - Everybody Loves a History by Kevin Eden
ISBN: 0946 719 07 1.
192 pages (illustrated). £9.95

A fascinating look at one of punk's most endearing and enduring bands, including interviews with all band members. A self-analysis of the complex motivations which have often seen the various members cross the boundaries between music and art.

"Any band or their fans could feel well served by a book like Eden's". **Vox**

"Eden delivers a sharp portrayal of the punk industry's behaviour, influence and morality". **Q magazine**

TAPE DELAY by Charles Neal
ISBN: 0946 719 02 0.
256 pages (illustrated). £11.95

Marc Almond, Cabaret Voltaire, Nick Cave, Chris & Cosey, Coil, Foetus, Neubauten, Non, The Fall, The The, Lydia Lunch, New Order, Psychic TV, Rollins, Sonic Youth, Swans, Test Department and many more...

"A virtual Who's Who of people who've done the most to drag music out of commercial confinement". **NME.**

"Intriguing and interesting". **Q magazine.**

THE CAN BOOK by Pascal Bussy
ISBN: 0946 719 05 5.
192 pages (illustrated). £8.95

A complete histoy of Krautrock supremos, including band member biographies, chronology and discography.

"If Can's music is a mystery, then this book will make you want to investigate further". **Q magazine**

"Bussy's account of the characters and chronology of Can is helpfully musicalogical for the fan and iced generously enough with information and anecdotes to attract the as yet unaligned". **Melody Maker**

Kraftwerk - Man, Machine and Music by Pascal Bussy
ISBN: 0946 719 09 8.
200 pages (illustrated). £11.95

Uniquely definitive account of Kraftwerk's history, delving beyond their publicity shunning exterior to reveal the full story behind one of the most influential bands in the history of rock music. Based on interviews with Ralf Hutter, Florian Schneider, Karl Bartos, Emil Schult and many more.

"Bussy engagingly explains why they are one of the few groups who've actually changed how music sounds". **Q magazine**

"I doubt this book will ever be bettered". **Vox**

Digital Gothic - A Critical Discography Of Tangerine Dream
by Paul Stump   ISBN: 0946 719 18 7.
160 pages (illustrated). £9.95

In this critical discography, music journalist Paul Stump picks his way through a veritable minefield of releases, determining both the explosive and those which fail to ignite. For the very first time Tangerine Dream's mammoth output is placed within an ordered perspective.

"It focuses fascinatingly on the pre-soporific roots of the group and their place in a cool electronic lineage which traces right up to Detroit techno". **Mojo**

"A stimulating companion to the group's music". **The Wire**

FORTHCOMING TITLES:

Captain Beefheart: Bill Harkleroad, formerly known as Zoot Horn Rollo in Beatheart's Magic Band, documents his years as the innovative guitarist on such classic albums as Trout Mask Replica and Clear Spot.
Due Autumn '97

If you find difficulty obtaining any title, all SAF books are stocked by, and are available mail order from:
Helter Skelter Bookshop, 4 Denmark Street, London WC2H 8LL Tel: 0171 836 1151 Fax: 0171 240 9880.

SAF Publishing Ltd

12 Conway Gardens, Wembley, Middx. HA9 8TR. England
Tel: +44 (0)181 904 6263 Fax: +44 (0)181 930 8565

Other titles available